PR
BITT

Bittersweet is so delicious I wanted to douse it in butter and syrup and eat the whole thing. I fell into a deep and genuine depression when I read the last word and there were no more. Be kind and please treat yourself to this book. It is lovely and hilarious and poignant in all the best ways that make me so deliriously happy as a reader.

JEN HATMAKER
speaker and author of *For the Love*
and *Of Mess and Moxie*

OTHER BOOKS
BY SHAUNA NIEQUIST

Cold Tangerines

Bread & Wine

Savor

Present Over Perfect

BITTERSWEET

THOUGHTS ON CHANGE, GRACE, AND LEARNING THE HARD WAY

SHAUNA NIEQUIST

ZONDERVAN
BOOKS

ZONDERVAN BOOKS

Bittersweet
Copyright © 2010, 2020 by Shauna Niequist

Requests for information should be addressed to:
Zondervan, *3900 Sparks Dr. SE, Grand Rapids, Michigan 49546*

Zondervan titles may be purchased in bulk for educational, business, fundrais-
ing, or sales promotional use. For information, please email SpecialMarkets@
Zondervan.com.

ISBN 978-0-310-36081-0 (softcover)

ISBN 978-0-310-59886-2 (audio)

ISBN 978-0-310-59885-5 (ebook)

The Library of Congress has cataloged the original/hardcover edition as follows:

Niequist, Shauna.
    Bittersweet : thoughts on change, grace, and learning the hard way /
Shauna Niequist.
      p. cm.
    ISBN 978-0-310-32816-2 (hardcover, printed) 1. Niequist, Shauna.
2. Christian biography. I. Title.
BR1725.N525A3 2010
277.3'083092—dc22 [B]   2010016554

Published in association with Yates & Yates, www.yates2.com.

Cover design: Curt Diepenhorst
Cover photo: ArtemSh / Shutterstock
Interior design: Kait Lamphere

Printed in the United States of America

20 21 22 23 24 25 26 27 28 /LSC/ 13 12 11 10 9 8 7 6 5 4 3 2 1

For Aaron—
most of what I've learned about love and about art,
I've learned from you.
You're the love story of my life.

CONTENTS

PREFACE

Today is the last school day of this year—of this decade, actually. It's the Friday before Christmas, bitterly cold, but the sky over Manhattan is clear blue. You can feel the swirl of the holidays all around. This morning, I went to our younger son's elementary school for a family breakfast. Together the parents and kids made a paper chain, one link each for something we're thankful for. Someone brought bagels and cream cheese, and someone else brought blueberries and bananas, and we brought juice, and everyone was extra grateful for whoever made a beautiful crumb cake—more crumb than cake, very much a hit with both parents and kids.

The kids were bouncing off the walls—from both the cake and the fact that it's the last day till winter break. The parents looked harried and tired. I felt harried and tired. But we made our paper chains, crouching down to be level with their tables, wielding glue sticks and markers.

What I'm thankful for today: For that third-grader and his brother, a seventh-grader. For their dad, my husband, Aaron. For a faith whose central stories are not of pomp and circumstance but a teenage couple, a baby, a star. Christmas is rapidly approaching, and with each passing year, I have less capacity for the sparkle and more affection for the simpler sounds and sights: a hymn, the bread my Aunt Mary makes every year, the Advent book we read every night before bed.

I wrote *Bittersweet* ten years ago—can that be? And when I reread it, I see a young woman who is longing for a sibling for her young son, and also longing for a sense of stability and safety in the world. She feels upended by everything she can't control, and through the writing of the book, she pushes more and more deeply into her faith, almost daring it to fail her, daring it to prove unable to hold the weight of her grief and fear. But it does hold. And more than that, it reshapes her heart page by page, and she becomes a little more faithful and a little less fearful along the way.

Ten years later, it all still rings true: a woman who wants more guarantees than life offers, who has learned the hard way that safety and stability are temporary states, and that change and discomfort are unavoidable parts of life as a grown-up. I don't think of myself as a change-averse person—until I have to do it, and then I'm forced to face the truth about myself, which is that I like change just fine, as long as it's completely on *my* terms and timelines. And maybe I'm not the only one.

What they say is true: The second book (or album or show or whatever) is always harder than the first, for at least two reasons. First, you've written all your best stories. The first book gets all the best material that you've been living and working out for your whole life, and then the second book gets, like, the next eighteen months of life and material. Inherently, this is not going to go well. You've left it all on the field, and now all of a sudden, there's supposed to be more to say about . . . anything?

The second reason it's harder is because now that you've written one book, you've been exposed to the truth of publishing, namely, that most of us are not, in fact, instant bestselling authors, and also that there are actual human people who hate our books and tell us all about it on the internet. Before the first book comes out, you can harbor this sweet, secret belief that you might be a genius and everyone's about to find out and also you might actually be the first and only person in history to write a book that is universally loved. This is impossible, but you don't have to face that fact till the first book is published.

Cold Tangerines, my first book, was a book about celebration—I can do that. I love that. That's my jam. And even though in the course of writing it I had to live through and then write through getting fired from a job I loved, and all the attending wounds and broken relationships surrounding it, I still knew where true north was: happiness, goodness, hope, celebration.

This book, though, felt like falling down a mineshaft. *Who wants to read this mess?* I wondered, over and over. As I neared the deadline, I kept hoping for hope, for good news, for if not a happy ending then at least one that wasn't quite so dire. But there was no happy ending. I wrote the epilogue through tears, almost apologetically—*I'm sorry, dear reader, that I can't give you what I wanted to give you.*

I wanted the ending to be beautiful, an unmistakable sign of hope. But I couldn't find one, and I couldn't pretend. The book did not end with hope, but it did end with comfort. I didn't have much hope, but I did have a sense of the comfort of Christ. I remember so clearly driving home at dusk one night just after that second miscarriage and almost whispering the phrase *Christ my comforter, Christ my comforter.* I whispered it under my breath over and over. Sometimes it helped.

I never wanted to be known for writing about miscarriage—that wasn't what I was intending to do in this book. But to this day, I get messages from all over the world that this book kept someone company while she was grieving, or this book was left on a front porch with a note attached, or this book stayed on a nightstand through the howling storms of miscarriage and infertility. I can't tell you what that means to me. If someone had asked me to write about getting through either of those things, I would have said, "Of course not—I'm not an expert. All I have is my own experience." Sometimes, though, that's enough to bridge the gap that needs to be bridged from one lonely, terrified heart to another.

This is the deal, it seems: when you decide to write or create art in any way, you have the honor and the challenge of connecting with people in the most tender parts of their own lives, writing from the most tender parts of your own.

I've been writing books for almost fifteen years, and for every one of those years, I have loved my work and have been so grateful to be an artist and a storyteller. But the single thing that has tripped me up more than any other part of it has been writing about my pain, particularly while it was still fresh, while it was still unfolding, while it still felt like there was a concrete block on my chest. But maybe that's part of the calling, even though I've resisted that part for so long.

Maybe this process—writing a new preface to an old book—is an invitation to accept the last piece of the puzzle, the last key to this wonderful, challenging vocation: that the most valuable part of what writers do is grapple with their own pain. As a reader, I know that's true. When I think about the memoirs, especially, that I've loved, it's the ones that have the howl, the despair, the glinting darkness.

Writing that matters, or that matters to me, is like sitting at a loom and unraveling each thread of your loss and your fear and your disillusionment and your loneliness, pulling it back and forth across the loom, over and over, each wound, each loss, until over time, those dark threads become a garment, a blanket that can be wrapped around a lonely person who desperately needs to know that they're not the first and not the last to feel bereft or terrified. In some seasons, I've resisted the requirements of it—scared by the depth of my own pain, daunted by the volume of critics, exhausted by the hours and years spent absorbing other people's opinions about my life.

But this is what I do. This is cosmic, spiritual recycling: I hold out my broken heart and God puts his hand on it, and in his grace, he allows it to be used in the repair of another heart, almost like a transplant, like a grafting, like a resurrection.

I don't go looking for pain. Even after everything I've learned about how sharing our pain transforms both the writer and the reader, I'm still more comfortable in the happy, sweet spaces. Maybe I always will be. But with each passing year, I try to get more comfortable in the dark. I do my best to allow my pain to be used in the healing and restoration of anyone who needs it.

When you're feeling joy and happiness and hope, it's easy to feel connected to people. You feel the collective rising joy all around you—color and happiness and cute children and blue skies. But pain, in my experience, is inherently isolating. There are two problems, then: your pain, and the loneliness you feel in that place of pain. Part of a writer's job is to offer up their own pain as a connection point for someone else. Offering up your joy is the easy part. Offering up your pain or confusion or loss—that's the calling part.

Bittersweet is still a word that resounds with me in such deep ways. It's a pleasing word to write and also to say out loud, and to a word person like me, that matters. It's also a word that captures so much about life, about the reality of a beautiful and broken world, about the interplay between darkness and light, about that knife-edge where joy and pain intersect in all our hearts.

I was naive enough when I wrote this book to believe that bittersweet would be a phase for me, a season, and then the normal part of life would resume—the sweet part. I believed that bittersweet was a temporary condition, an aberration.

Since that time, I've been through some seasons that were almost entirely bitter, where sweetness was nowhere to be found, nights that were so dark my eyes never adjusted and so long I almost lost hope that dawn would ever come.

Now I know that bittersweet is where we spend most of our lives—if we're lucky, that is. I was young enough and inexperienced enough with loss and heartache to believe that they were anomalies, and now I know that fear and pain are woven right into the very fabric of our world, of our lives. This is how it is. There's goodness. And there's wreckage. There's joy. And there's betrayal. There's beauty. And there's destruction.

This is life. This is bittersweet. This is how it is—most of the time for most of us.

And if this is true, then we might as well try to get comfortable here, here in the dark and light, the beautiful and terrible territory, here in the land of bittersweet. It's not a neighborhood, like I thought it was, something to drive through quickly on your way to the next uncomplicated happiness. It's a land where most of us will spend most of our lives, and so let's learn to live well in it, to tell the truth about it, to stare it down instead of looking away. To celebrate what we can when we can, but also to get comfortable with the language of sorrow.

If you find yourself in the territory of bittersweet, please know that you're not alone, and that even though it may not seem like it at first, it's not so bad here. It's not sparkly or simple. It's not shiny or perfect. But this is a place where good things grow, fertile soil for resilience, forgiveness, peace, courage. This is where you can sit shoulder to shoulder with people who've struggled just as you're struggling now. This is where God does his best work, his most tender healing, most breathtaking transformations. This is bittersweet.

Shauna Niequist
December 20, 2019
New York, New York

prologue

BITTERSWEET

The idea of *bittersweet* is changing the way I live, unraveling and reweaving the way I understand life. Bittersweet is the idea that in all things there is both something broken and something beautiful, that there is a sliver of lightness on even the darkest of nights, a shadow of hope in every heartbreak, and that rejoicing is no less rich when it contains a splinter of sadness.

Bittersweet is the practice of believing that we really do need both the bitter and the sweet, and that a life of nothing but sweetness rots both your teeth and your soul. Bitter is what makes us strong, what forces us to push through, what helps us earn the lines on our faces and the calluses on our hands. Sweet is nice enough, but bittersweet is beautiful, nuanced, full of depth and complexity. Bittersweet is courageous, gutsy, earthy.

Nearly ten years ago, my friend Doug told me that the central image of the Christian faith is death and rebirth, that the core of it all, over and over again, is death and rebirth. I'm sure I'd heard that before, but when he told me, for whatever reason, I really thought about it for the first time. And at the time, I didn't agree.

What I didn't understand until recently is that he wasn't speaking to me as a theologian or a pastor or an expert, but rather as a person whose heart had been broken and who had been brought back to life by the story God tells in all our lives. When you haven't yet had your heart really broken, the gospel isn't about death and rebirth. It's about life and more life. It's about hope and possibility and a brighter future. And it is, certainly, about those things.

But when you've faced some kind of death—the loss of someone you loved dearly, the failure of a dream, the fracture of a relationship—that's when you start understanding that central metaphor. When your life is easy, a lot of the really crucial parts of Christian doctrine and life are nice theories, but you don't really need them. When, however, death of any kind is staring you in the face, all of a sudden rebirth and new life are very, very important to you.

Now, ten years later, I know Doug was right. I've thought about his words a thousand times in the last few years, a season in my own life that has felt in some moments like death at every turn. I've begun to train my eyes for rebirth, like looking for buds on branches after an endlessly long winter. I know that death is real, and I trust that rebirth is real, too.

Christians, generally, aren't great at lament and mourning. Jews are really better at lament, maybe because they've had more practice. My favorite part of a Jewish wedding is the breaking of the glass. Like most Jewish traditions, there are a whole bunch of interpretations: some say that all the shards of broken glass suggest loads of future children and future happiness. Some say that the breaking of the glass references the irreversible nature of marriage: in the same way that the glass can never be put back together after it's been broken, two people can never be separated once they've been connected by marriage. But my favorite interpretation is the one where the wine in the glass is a symbol for all of life, and when the bride and groom drink it, they accept both the bitter and the sweet aspects of life. They accept that sometimes they'll celebrate and sometimes they'll mourn, in the same way that sometimes they'll drink wine and sometimes glasses will shatter.

This collection is an ode to all things bittersweet, to life at the edges, a love letter to what change can do in us. This is what I've come to believe about change: it's good, in the way that childbirth is good, and heartbreak is good, and failure is good. By that I mean that it's incredibly painful, exponentially more so if you fight it, and also that it has the potential to open you up, to open life up, to deliver you right into the palm of God's hand, which is where you wanted to be all along, except that you were too busy pushing and pulling your life into exactly what you thought it should be.

So this is the work I'm doing now, and the work I invite you into: when life is sweet, say thank you and celebrate. And when life is bitter, say thank you and grow.

one

LEARNING TO SWIM

I learned about waves when I was little, swimming in Lake Michigan in navy blue water under a clear sky, and the most important thing I learned was this: if you try to stand and face the wave, it will smash you to bits, but if you trust the water and let it carry you, there's nothing sweeter. And a couple decades later, that's what I'm learning to be true about life, too. If you dig in and fight the change you're facing, it will indeed smash you to bits. It will hold you under, drag you across the rough sand, scare and confuse you.

This last season in my life has been characterized, more than anything else, by change. Hard, swirling, one-after-another changes, so many that I can't quite regain my footing before the next one comes, very much like being tumbled by waves. It began three years ago, in January in Grand Rapids, Michigan. I got pregnant, lost a job I loved, had a baby, wrote a book. A year after I lost my job, my husband, Aaron, left his job in a really painful way, and then for the next year and a half we traveled together and separately almost every week, doing all the freelance work we could find, looking for a new home and trying to pay the bills. Leaving our jobs at the church meant leaving the church community, the heart of our world in Grand Rapids, and that loss left a hole in our lives that was as tender and palpable as a bruise.

The day after our son Henry's first birthday, my brother Todd left on a two-year sailing trip around the world, taking my husband's best friend Joe with him. My best friend, Annette, left Grand Rapids and moved back to California. I got pregnant again, our kitchen and basement flooded, and on the Fourth of July I lost the baby. My first thought, there in the doctor's office, was, *Everything in my life is dying. I can't keep anything alive.*

At some point in all that, we put our house up for sale, which meant lots and lots of showings but no offers. After several months, my husband and our son and I left our house still for sale and moved home to Chicago, to a little house on the same street I lived on as a child, exhausted and battered, out of breath and shaken up.

It may appear to an outside observer that these have been the best years of our lives. We became parents to a healthy child; we met interesting people and heard their stories and were welcomed into their homes and churches. I wrote a book, and Aaron recorded an album, and we got to be, really and truly, working artists. Every time I read over that list, I know that it should have been wonderful. But *should have been* is worth absolutely nothing. For most of that season, I was clenching my teeth, waiting for impact, longing for it to be over.

I know that to another person my difficult season would have been a walk in the park, and that all over the world, people suffer in unimaginable ways and manage far worse than my own little list.

I was miserable because I lost touch with the heart of the story, the part where life always comes from death. I love the life part, and I always try to skip over that pesky death part. You can't do that, as much as I've tried.

I believe that God is making all things new. I believe that Christ overcame death and that pattern is apparent all through life and history: life from death, water from a stone, redemption from failure, connection from alienation. I believe that suffering is part of the narrative, and that nothing really good gets built when everything's easy. I believe that loss and emptiness and confusion often give way to new fullness and wisdom.

But for a long season, I forgot all those things. I didn't stop believing in God. It wasn't a crisis of faith. I prayed and served and pursued a life of faith the way I had before that season and the way I still do now. But I realized all at once, sitting in church on a cold dark night, that the story I was telling was the wrong one—or at the very least, an incomplete one. I had been telling the story about how hard it was. That's not the whole story. The rest of the story is that I failed to live with hope and courage and lived instead a long season of whining, self-indulgence, and fear. This is my confession.

I'm able to see now that what made that season feel so terrible to me were not the changes. What made that season feel so terrible is that I lost track of some of the crucial beliefs and practices that every Christian must carry with them. Possibly a greater tragedy is that I didn't even know it until much later.

Looking back now I can see that it was more than anything a failure to believe in the story of who God is and what he is doing in this world. Instead of living that story—one of sacrifice and purpose and character—I began to live a much smaller story, and that story was only about me. I wanted an answer, a timeline, and a map. I didn't want to have to trust God or anything I couldn't see. I didn't want to wait or follow. I wanted my old life back, and even while I read the mystics and the prophets, even while I prayed fervently, even while I sat in church and begged for God to direct my life, those things didn't have a chance to transform me, because under those actions and intentions was a rocky layer of faithlessness, fear, and selfishness.

I believe that faith is less like following a GPS through a precise grid of city blocks, and more like being out at sea: a tricky journey, nonlinear and winding, the wind kicking up and then stalling. But what I really wanted in the middle of it all was some dry land and a computer-woman's soothing voice leading me through the mess.

If I'm honest, I prayed the way you order breakfast from a short-order cook: This is what I want. Period. This is what I want. Aren't you getting this? I didn't pray for God's will to be done in my life, or, at any rate, I didn't mean it. I prayed to be rescued, not redeemed. I prayed for it to get easier, not that I would be shaped in significant ways. I prayed for the waiting to be over, instead of trying to learn something about patience or anything else for that matter.

I couldn't make peace with uncertainty—but there's nothing in the biblical narrative that tells us certainty is part of the deal. I couldn't unclench my hands and my jaw, and I locked my knees and steeled myself in the face of almost every wave. I cried in the shower and alone in my car. When I looked into my own eyes in the mirror, they seemed flat and lifeless, and things that should have been wonderful left me blank and despairing. Sometimes at parties during that season, I felt my cheeks trying to smile, but I knew that my eyes weren't playing along. The tension and anxiety flattened me, and the fear about our future threatened to vacuum up the energy and buoyancy from almost every day, even as I fought to celebrate the good moments. Looking back, it seems like I mostly lost that fight, or possibly, generously, it was a draw.

Every wave presents us with a choice to make, and quite often, unfortunately, I have stood, both resolute and terrified, staring down a wave. I have been smacked straight on with the force of the water, tumbled, disoriented, gasping for breath and for my swimsuit bottoms, and spit onto shore, embarrassed and sand-burned, standing up only to get knocked down again, refusing to float on the surface and surrender to the sea.

There were also a few glittering, very rare moments of peace and sweetness, when I felt the goodness and familiarity of people who loved me, when God's voice sounded tender and fatherly to my ears, when I was able to release my breath and my fists for just a moment and float. And as I mine back through my heart and memories, I notice something interesting: the best moments of the last few years were the very rare moments when I've allowed these changes to work their way through my life, when I've lived up to my faith, when I've been able even for a minute to see life as more than my very own plan unfolding on my schedule, when I've practiced acceptance, when I've floated instead of fought, when I've rested, even for a moment, on the surface instead of wrestling the water itself. And those moments are like heaven.

So that's where my mind and heart are these days: more moments of heaven, and less locking of the knees. More awareness of God's presence and action and ability, and less stranglehold on my fear and anxiety. More floating, and less getting tumbled.

And while I certainly didn't thrive in the process, I'm really thankful for the result. I'm thankful for what change forced me to face within myself. I found myself confronted by the whiny, entitled child I had become. I like what got stripped away—like my expectations—and what was revealed. I appreciate the things that became grounded more deeply in my spirit and in my marriage. I respect the things that change forged in my life, even though it was very painful.

More than anything, I know now that I never want to live that way again—I don't like the person I became, and I'm not proud of the contagious fear and ugliness I left in my wake everywhere I went. Again, this is my confession, and my promise: I want to live a new way, the way I've always believed, but temporarily lost sight of.

I know now that I can make it through more than I thought, with less than I thought. I know better than to believe that the changes are over, and I know better than to believe the next ones will be easier, but I've learned the hard way that change is one of God's greatest gifts and one of his most useful tools. I've learned the hard way that change can push us, pull us, rebuke and remake us. It can show us who we've become, in the worst ways, and also in the best ways. I've learned that it's not something to run away from, as though we could, and I've learned that in many cases, change is not a function of life's cruelty but instead a function of God's graciousness.

The world is changing all the time, at every moment. Someone is falling in love right now, and someone is being born. A dream is coming true in some city or small town, and right at the same moment, another dream is crashing and crumbling. A marriage is ending somewhere, and it's somebody's wedding day, maybe even right in the same town. It's all happening.

If you dig in and fight the changes, they will smash you to bits. They'll hold you under, drag you across the rough sand, scare and confuse you. But if you can find it within yourself, in the wildest of seasons, just for a moment, to trust in the goodness of God, who made it all and holds it all together, you'll find yourself drawn along to a whole new place, and there's truly nothing sweeter. Unclench your fists, unlock your knees and also the door to your heart, take a deep breath, and begin to swim. Begin to let the waves do their work in you.

two

THE BLUE HOUSE

In July two summers ago, Aaron led worship at our church in Grand Rapids for the last time. Many of our dearest friends came to the evening service, and although I cried steadily through it, I felt surrounded in a very deep way, shoulder to shoulder with our friends Annette and Joe, catching eyes with my dad and my brother Todd.

For a year after I lost my job at the same church, Aaron stayed in his job there. It was tricky, and by that I mean it was okay sometimes but desperately awkward and raw at other times. Over time it became harder and harder for Aaron to love his job.

When we moved there five years earlier, that church had quickly become Aaron's spiritual home, a place that represented deep hope, redemption, possibility. After years of cynicism and suspicion about the church as an institution, he gave himself to this one wholly. And then at a certain point, because it changed and he changed and a million other things shifted and broke, he realized that what had connected him so deeply to this church no longer existed there. His leaving felt surreal, and like history was repeating itself in a funhouse mirror— different from my leaving in all sorts of ways, but similar, too, dredging up memories and still-unresolved sadness.

After that last service, Aaron and I walked out of the building alone. He carried with him a little box of the last few things left in his office. There are times when the actual experience of leaving something makes you wish desperately that you could stay, and then there are times when the leaving reminds you a hundred times over why exactly you had to leave in the first place, and this was one of those. We drove home in silence and began packing, more than ready to leave that town and all those memories for a little while.

One of the best and worst parts of working at a big church in a small town is that everywhere you go, you see someone you know. When things fell apart for us at the church, the town felt even smaller than it actually was, with stilted inter-actions and overly personal questions and conspiracy theories every time we went out for dinner or to the grocery store.

The morning after that last service, we moved from Grand Rapids to South Haven, a tiny lakeshore town an hour from Grand Rapids where my family has been spending summers all my life. Some friends let us stay in their lovely blue house there for the summer, to be near my family and take a deep breath as we figured out what was next. The freelance work we were both doing didn't require offices, and we sure didn't want to be in Grand Rapids right then, so we jumped at the opportunity.

We were so happy to be in South Haven, away from all the chaos and pain. We didn't realize till months later that we were like ghosts, there but not there, heartbroken and reeling while we pushed the stroller to the farmer's market or to the pier. We threw parties and had weekend guests and grilled out, but in our bedroom or in our car driving up to a party or as we strolled Henry all around town, we cried bitter tears and snapped at each other, both of us confused and lonely and scared.

We kept ourselves in the blur and busyness of entertaining and houseguests because we wanted to share that beautiful house and because we missed our friends, and underneath it all, because we were afraid to slow down, to rattle around in that house alone, far from anything that even resembled a plan for the future. So we kept moving, kept entertaining. Looking back, it's as though we were shadows in that house that summer, absent in the most important way. Eating fresh blueberries and peppery arugula from the farmer's market, drinking chardonnay on the porch, and stripping beds and folding towels: busy, but not there.

One more set of weekend guests, one more load of sheets and towels, one more salad, one more boat ride, one more walk to the pier at sunset. We were the tour guides, the travel bureau, the chef and the maid, the boat captain and first mate. We pointed out local sights, recommended restaurants, packed and unpacked the cooler, loaded and unloaded the dishwasher, and all the while, we knew that we were doing good things but not the best thing, not the very thing we needed. What we needed was to stop, to be alone and alone together, to be quiet verging on bored, to be silent enough to hear our lives changing.

Instead of walking together through the mess, talking and

listening, learning and hearing, Aaron and I squared off like boxers, demanding and bickering and then eventually just ignoring each other and attending to our guests. Another boat ride, anyone? More salad?

For the first time in our marriage, we wanted the exact opposite things. More than anything, Aaron wanted space and freedom—time to think, to heal, to retreat a little bit before diving into the next thing. Freelancing to him felt safe, because he couldn't be hurt by a church again if he didn't commit to a church again.

More than anything, I wanted a plan. I wanted to move, find a new church, start over as soon as possible. I hated the loneliness of traveling so much for work and felt unanchored without a church community. I felt like we were treading water, stuck in a life that was no longer livable, hanging on to the past. I was worried about neither of us having a paycheck, and Aaron was worried about jumping into the next thing just for a paycheck. The more worried I got, the more remote he got. We began a terrible dance at that blue house, and continued dancing it for the better part of a year.

Our inability to hear and understand one another was the worst part of this dark season, and that first summer was just the beginning. I regret my unwillingness to hear and understand my husband, and my rampant, illogical fear about our future. The two, of course, are related: if I hadn't been so wound up about a plan, maybe I would have been able to listen to him tell me that it wasn't flakiness but his own fears that kept him from moving forward. We found that fear is like a hand grenade: surprisingly powerful and surprisingly destructive.

Now a few years later, we're packing to go to that same house even as I write, piles around the house beginning to take shape: beach towels, books, jars of peanut butter, and bottles of wine. Our life has changed in a thousand ways since that summer, and my prayer for this summer is that Aaron and I will do now what we couldn't do then, that we'll face one another with tenderness and patience, that we'll let the house sit empty except for us sometimes, and let ourselves sit on the porch in the fading light hearing nothing but each other's voices.

I don't know what our future will hold, but I want us to walk together better than we did last time we were in that house. I want to build a new history in that same house, to exorcise the demons we left there last time. I want to dance together in the living room this time, instead of sitting on opposite sides of the couch, numbed by the TV, thankful that we don't have to talk. I want to remember more than endless amounts of laundry and hot silences. I want to feel present, like I'm feeding people out of love instead of desperation, like I've gathered people around the table in order to care for them, instead of as a way of insulating myself from our own mess. I'm thankful for a second chance there, and for all the second chances Aaron and I have been given since our first summer in that lovely blue house.

three

THE CLOSER YOU GET

I've been thinking about this night, about this exact moment, for months. I know every detail and every moment of what this night will be: housechurch dinner on a Wednesday night, just like always. Aaron and I, Annette and Andrew, Steve and Sarah—this time missing Joe.

When everyone arrives, Henry and Spence will run around the coffee table in their jammies—maybe the matching chocolate brown ones with the bulldogs. Maybe they'll even dance, Spence kind of running in place and Henry doing his Bill Cosby/penguin dance. Aaron will have chosen the music: Feist, maybe, or Arcade Fire or Spoon.

While we eat, we'll talk about the week over the boys' yelps and clatters. Tonight we're having mango chicken curry, a special occasion meal, the one Steve always requests on his birthday. I love it, but there's a whole lot of chopping involved, thus the special occasion designation.

Just like always, Aaron will tease Annette, and Steve will update us on his travels, and Andrew on his work, and Sarah on the baby and on painting. We'll talk about Joe, piecing together each of our brief conversations with him as he travels with my brother, Todd.

I can see the dimensions of this night in my mind before it happens because we've done it a hundred times. We've sat at this table, or Annette and Andrew's table, Joe's table, Steve and Sarah's table, with these faces and these sounds and tastes, for hundreds of nights. And tonight is the last time.

Tomorrow Annette and her family will leave, and all of life will change as they do. I remember when Annette called to tell me that she was offered the job in California, officially. It was a beautiful day, hot for October. It was the day before Henry's first birthday, and two days before Joe and Todd left on a sailing trip around the world, one they'd been planning for months. I stood out on the back patio and talked with her, pacing back and forth between the kitchen door and the grill, listening. I was so excited for her on the phone. I felt proud and excited and certain that this was the best thing, that life was opening up and leading her by the hand.

And then an hour later, I was putting towels away in the upstairs bathroom and began to cry so hard I bent over the sink and gripped it with both hands, and I watched my tears drop onto the white porcelain.

While Annette and Andrew were in California finding an apartment, I picked Spence up at his little school, and when he saw me he ran toward me and hugged me. We chatted in the car, about Henry and crackers and juice. Just before bedtime, both boys climbed up on the coffee table and danced to an old Green Day song.

I put Spence in his jammies and took him into Henry's room for a minute to rock him, and while I rocked him, I started to cry. This boy whom I watched grow day by day in my best friend's belly, this boy whom I held in the hospital, this boy for whom I brought diapers (with emergency ice cream for Andrew) in the blurry first days of his life, this boy is going to California, too. This boy is one of the miracles this recent season has given us.

When I picked Spence up from school, his teacher asked me if I was a relative. I am not. But if family status is measured in love, I am. He is not my boy, but he is the only other boy I rock to sleep, whose diaper I change, whom I feed and kiss and care for. And that night, in the dim light as I rocked him and sang to him, the enormity of my very best friend's leaving became real to me.

It reminded me of the day Annette and I realized that Spence knew his way from her house to ours, and that he could run the whole way. How entirely fitting it is that his first destination was Henry's house: Paris Avenue to Hoyt, across Madison to Aurora.

How many nights did we spend on Annette's upstairs porch, watching the light fade, listening to the barking dogs in the distance? How many times did we go to the Real Food Café? And how many times did she order her toast dry, and then ask for butter? How many late nights in South Haven or Saugatuck, how many mornings at Uncommon Grounds? How many times did we deliver dinner back and forth, or maternity clothes or baby clothes or maybe-it-will-fit-you-but-it-doesn't-fit-me clothes? How many times did we walk back and forth from Paris, along Hoyt, across Madison, and over to Aurora?

Of all the things, of all the thousands of memories and snapshots of our lives together, from college to trips to weddings to the last three years in Grand Rapids, there is one thing that rises above everything else like a siren, like a smoke signal. It's this: the closer you get, the closer you get. I didn't always know how to open myself deeply. Moving to Grand Rapids, a town that was tricky for me for all sorts of reasons, and the fear and the loneliness of it, snapped my heart shut like a drum.

And then Annette and Andrew moved across the country and into our neighborhood and day by day, phone call by phone call, breakfast by breakfast, Annette taught me that the closer you get, the closer you get. That when you allow someone past all the doors you were taught to keep closed, what you find behind those doors is a kind of friendship I didn't even have a category for. I've spent most of my life and most of my friendships holding my breath and hoping that when people get close enough they won't leave, and fearing that it's a matter of time before they figure me out and go.

And every time I told Annette the truth, or asked for something difficult, or opened a scary conversation, when I thought she would back away, she walked forward. And by walking forward, she changed me, and now, everywhere I go, everywhere life takes me, I'll be looking for this, for this kind of friendship that my dear friend Annette taught me.

I remember sitting around the table with the housechurch and my parents on my thirtieth birthday, long after we'd finished eating, telling stories and laughing together. At one point my dad said, "You know this doesn't happen over and over in your life. You don't get that many experiences of friendship like the ones you all share." We nodded, thankful in that moment. But I think we wanted to believe he was wrong, and that friendships like these would pop up all over our lives like dandelions.

Now having said goodbye, we know that he was right, and that the richness and connectedness of that season was indeed rare. We said our first goodbye to Joe when he left on the sailing trip in October, our sadness softened by the knowledge that he'd be back. Then just when his absence stopped being quite so raw, we said goodbye to Annette and Andrew the week before Christmas. I wish I could tell you that sadness has softened, but it hasn't, and I'll never forget the actual terrible moment of goodbye.

The day after the housechurch dinner, after they packed the car and closed up the house, Annette called and said, "We're ready. Come over." Aaron and I were on our way to Chicago for Christmas, so with our own car packed and Henry wriggling in his car seat, Aaron pulled our car into their driveway as Annette came out the side door. We hugged in the freezing cold, not knowing where to start, not knowing what to say. Finally she said, "I love you. Go." I got in the car and cried till we got to the lake, and Aaron didn't even try to stop me.

And so Annette and Andrew and Spence, no matter where you are in the world, no matter where life takes you, you will always be as close in our hearts, as the very short walk from Paris, along Hoyt, across Madison, and over to Aurora.

four

WHAT WE ATE AND WHY IT MATTERS

During this last season, one thing I remember more clearly than anything else is what we ate. The undercurrent of our life was dark and ragged, but my senses remember so much beauty, too, possibly the soul's way of finding balance or hope. All those flavors and textures and smells are still embedded in my memories, and that feels like a gift.

My brother's memory works mostly in terms of cars. I'll say, "Remember my friend Monica from college?" And he'll say, "Yeah, red Nissan truck?" Monica hasn't driven that truck for a decade, but now Todd knows who I'm talking about. It's how my husband is with music: all of life linked to the soundtrack playing in his memory. And that's how I am with food.

When I think about a weekend in Kansas City last summer, my first memory is a Z-Man sandwich from Oklahoma

Joe's, and the way the sun slanted across Kevin and Katie's table as we ate foil-wrapped bundles of spicy meat and crispy French fried onions. When I think about Hollywood and my friend Laura, I think of bacon-wrapped dates from Cobras and Matadors and drinking peppery, plummy red wine out of tiny glasses.

And more than the food I've eaten in restaurants, I remember the food I've prepared with my own hands. I'm by no means a great cook, and I have a terrible habit of not using recipes. Sometimes my mother has to leave the kitchen when I'm cooking, because things get a little chaotic, and my lack of technique leaves a bit to be desired, but I really believe that every person should be able to feed themselves and the people they love. I think preparing food and feeding people brings nourishment not only to our bodies but to our spirits. Feeding people is a way of loving them, in the same way that feeding ourselves is a way of honoring our own createdness and fragility.

When we stop everything else to gather around the table and eat a meal made by someone's hands, we honor our bodies and the God who created them. We honor the world he made and the beauty of creation. And in that moment we acknowledge that even though life is fast and frantic, we're not machines and we do require nourishment, physically and otherwise.

We're living in a funny time right now, when people build restaurant-grade kitchens in their homes, and if you walk into a specialty cooking store, it seems like you need sixteen gadgets and a graduate degree to make a meal. At the same time, other people live entirely on takeout, frozen food, and energy bars that don't resemble anything close to food. I think there's a middle ground worth finding between those two extremes, where we feed ourselves and the people we love with our hands and without a lot of tricks and fanfare.

I learned to cook largely because of our housechurch. The rules were strict: when you're hosting, you do everything—cooking, table-setting, dessert, clean up. But when it's not your house, you don't lift a finger. You show up and eat. Another rule: takeout is totally acceptable, as are experiments that might result in last-minute takeout anyway.

We know, after years of dinners, that Aaron eats gluten-free, Sarah doesn't eat red meat or shrimp, and for that group you can never go wrong with Mexican food. We know that Andrew eats very, very slowly and has an insatiable sweet tooth, Steve dislikes lots of things but is too polite to tell us, and Joe, more than anyone, appreciates any attempt at fancy plating, because although he'll deny it, during one season in his life he watched a whole lot of Food Network.

For anyone who wants to overcome either a cooking or entertaining phobia, I recommend a weekly dinner gathering wholeheartedly. I think we happened into a truly beautiful system. Knowing that you have to cook for a bunch of people every few weeks keeps you in the rhythm, keeps the stakes pretty low, and keeps your eyes open for something yummy all the time.

When we began we were, admittedly, showing off. We made our best recipes, set our most lavish tables, hit after hit each week. But then after six or so rotations, we realized we were out of hits. We'd had Annette's almond chicken and her enchiladas, Sarah's calzones and chicken with queso fresca, and my lasagna, curry, and barbecue chicken chopped salad. One of the best meals we ever had was Joe's doing, and it involved a grilled fresh peach sauce over chicken and a sweet corn salad that was just fantastic.

After we played all our best cards, we had to start experimenting. And that's really how you learn, by giving it a shot and taking risks and learning with your hands and your nose and your mouth. That season yielded some lovely experiments and some total disasters, and you need both along the way.

If I learned to cook in Grand Rapids, I love cooking most in South Haven. In the summers there, some days I feel like the farmer's market is a whole cookbook waiting to be cooked— green beans blanched, tossed with marcona almonds, feta, and raspberries. Tomatoes with basil and salt and pepper and a really vinegary dressing. Baby greens with Dijon vinaigrette. Polenta with tomato sauce, mozzarella, black olives, and basil leaves. White freestone peaches grilled with ice cream and warm caramel sauce.

Summer tastes like big salads with arugula and feta and blueberries, the tang of the cheese balancing the sweetness of the berries. Sometimes we add chicken from the grill, or pears, or diced candied ginger or sweet corn or heirloom tomatoes, but always the peppery greens, the creamy bite of the cheese, and the rich blue summer-taste of blueberries, bought in a five-pound box at the farmer's market, washed and left in the colander on the counter, to be eaten by the handful every time we walk by.

Many of the most deeply spiritual moments of my life haven't happened just in my mind or in my soul. They happened while holding my son in the middle of the night, or watching the water break along the shore, or around my table, watching the people I love feel nourished in all sorts of ways.

From my vantage point, the idea that faith and meaning and all the other important things happen in your mind or soul where no one can see them is one of the worst by-products of modern Christianity. We are, whether we choose to acknowledge it or not, physical beings. And *physical* isn't negative. If we didn't have bodies, we couldn't feel the sun on our faces or smell the earthy, mushroomy rich smell of the ground right after the rain. If we didn't have bodies, we couldn't wrap our arms around the people we love or taste a perfect tomato right at the height of summer. I'm so thankful to live in this physical, messy, blood-and-guts world. I don't want to live in a world that's all dry ideas and theorems. Food is one of the ways we acknowledge our humanity, our appetites, our need for nourishment. And so it may seem trivial or peripheral to some people, but to me, when I'm telling a story, the part about what we ate really does matter.

five

HEARTBEAT

I had a miscarriage in early July when I was just over eleven weeks pregnant. We'd found out I was pregnant on Memorial Day weekend, and I was sicker than I'd been with Henry. We didn't plan on telling Aaron's extended family until I was a little further along, but when I threw up behind our car at a family party, they knew. I barely fit into my dress at my friend Betsy's birthday party, and could hardly keep my eyes open at dinner, enveloped in the total haze of the first trimester.

Everything felt different this time, and I had been worried at several points. On a bright Wednesday morning, I called the doctor so I could put my nagging fears to rest. They fit me in that day, so Aaron and I drove up from the lake to the doctor's office in Grand Rapids. One appointment led to another, and we went from the office to an ultrasound to the lab for blood work to the hospital for another ultrasound.

What began as a mild morning became a steel-colored

sky and then a hailstorm, and while we were waiting between appointments, we pulled over the car on a downtown street to watch the hail fall on the windshield and the rivers of rainwater run down the street. The power was out, and the wind was whipping, and it felt exactly appropriate for the events of the day. We showed up at our last appointment soaking wet, partially from the rain, and partially because I'd been crying for hours, watching the doctors' faces become more impassive throughout the day. Impassive, for doctors, is always a bad sign.

We saw a new doctor that day, and even though she didn't look old enough to order a drink in a bar, over the next several days, we appreciated her skill, her kindness, and her phone calls, providing information and asking if we were all right. I remember clutching the phone, hoping every time. And even though the news she gave us was never good news, hearing her voice always made me feel like the ground was stable, even if just for a minute.

I had surgery early in the morning on Friday, the Fourth of July. When Aaron brought me back to the lake, I took pain medication and watched the fireworks from the couch. Our friends called and stopped by and blew kisses from the boats as they passed. I was absolutely shocked by the physical pain, and what I didn't realize until later was that the physical pain absorbed me so fully that it shielded me for a while from the deeper feelings of loss and emptiness.

I didn't have a "normal" miscarriage, as though it ever feels normal to anyone. Mine was a molar pregnancy, and that had a few strange implications. Among them, even after the surgery, my pregnancy hormones were still twenty times what they should have been. In the midst of the recovery, I was still very nauseous, and I threw up three times on Monday, with Henry standing in the bathroom doorway watching me. It seemed like a cruel joke that I was no longer pregnant, but still so sick.

The molar pregnancy also meant that I absolutely couldn't try to have another baby for at least six full months, and that I had monthly and sometimes weekly blood work and frequent x-rays and ultrasounds. It also put me into the high-risk category, and having had one molar pregnancy, there's a high chance I'll have another. No one I knew had ever heard of a molar pregnancy, and all of a sudden we were sorting through excerpts from medical journals, trying to wrap our minds around this new reality.

I was okay, and not okay. I changed diapers and folded laundry and wrote. And I had bad dreams and woke to find my face wet with tears several nights in a row, and I flinched every time I saw the date on the calendar, the date that would have been the due date. What will we do on that day? What will life be like on that day? How do you mark a birthday that isn't a birthday at all?

When I look back at that time, what I remember more clearly than anything were the hours I spent reading on our tiny balcony looking out at the river, and the late morning trips to the farmer's market. For whatever reason, those were the two things that made me feel normal again, that healed me slowly. In the early mornings, I read on the balcony as morning broke, quietly at first, and then with vigor, as the beer trucks arrived and the kegs for the bar across the street bounced and rolled down the cobblestones.

I went to the farmer's market every chance I got, for heavy black cherries and fingerling potatoes and bunches of radishes.

The smell of dirt and herbs seemed like the essence of life, something I needed desperately. In some moments, it seemed to me that the stalls of that market were more sacred and nourishing than any church I'd ever been to, like life itself was there, reaching out to me, with dirty fingers like carrots.

As I told people what had happened, I heard more and more of the same terrible song in the same minor melody. One in three or four pregnancies ends the way mine did, and all of a sudden, I was surrounded by stories. People I'd known for years told me stories I'd never heard about their own miscarriages, and that helped in ways I never could have understood before. People with big, healthy families have stories just like mine, and it gave me a little bit of hope that this is not the end of our story, that life and health can follow the emptiness I felt so acutely in those moments.

For the first few months, I froze just for a split second when I saw pregnant women, the way you do when you see someone who just broke up with you from across the room at a crowded party. For almost three months, I was one of them, and felt all the solidarity and connection that goes with being a pregnant woman. And now pregnant women don't want anything to do with me, and don't want to hear my story, because I'm that thing they're afraid could happen to them. I was so like them, and now I'm so deeply not.

I understand, a little, why people sometimes have memorial services after miscarriages. You wake up from surgery, and it's over. There's no gathering of friends and family, no prayers, no final moment when you walk away from a grave. I emerged from anesthesia, and it was over. Theoretically, it was over. Medically, it was over. But a medical procedure didn't put this life to rest, as much as I hoped it would. The wounds still felt open, and I didn't know what to do to close them.

It's easy to believe that having a child is as simple as growing tomatoes: you do the right couple things, you take your prenatals and avoid caffeine and nitrates, and the universe hands you a perfect life, right on schedule. But if you've ever tried to grow anything—a tomato plant, a baby, anything—you know it's more mysterious and more treacherous than that. It turns out that conceiving and carrying a healthy baby is just exactly like a lot of other parts of life: way more out of our control than we prefer to believe. There's a mystery we tend not to acknowledge until certainty has been ripped out of our clutching hands. And only when certainty is gone do we allow ourselves to bend and open to that terrifying mystery, dark and incomprehensible.

There is, right now, no little baby heartbeat inside me. But there is still inside my ribs my own beating heart. Battered and raw, my tired old heart, but beating. And every beat reminds me that my own life is unfolding, and my own heart will keep on beating, even if its beating is singular for now. I look for life everywhere I can find it, sustained by the rhythm of my own lonely heartbeat, the smell of rosemary, the sound of Henry's breathing as he sleeps.

six

ON DESPERATION
AND COLD PIZZA

Aaron, Henry, and I came back to our house in Grand Rapids at the end of August. Sometime during the summer, in a process so gradual it could almost be considered imperceptible, we decided to move back to Chicago. We didn't actually decide all in one moment. We sort of wandered closer and closer to the option until it became real, like squatter's rights or a common-law marriage. We got used to it, and realized that it felt like our future, with all the familiarity of favorite shoes. It wasn't an epiphany or a glamorous moment, even though we'd been longing for both for over a year. It just developed like a photograph, slowly and incrementally, after a full year of wondering and waiting.

Aaron had been invited to interview for a job at the church where I grew up, the church where we met and worked together until we moved to Grand Rapids. The decisions weren't yet made, on their end or on our end, and part of the way I dealt with the waiting, apparently, is by throwing our home into total, complete chaos.

Just after we came back to our house, construction began on our kitchen and basement, repairs from a flood earlier in the summer. For several weeks we washed sippy cups and coffee cups in the upstairs bathroom every night, or, if I was feeling really lazy, on the front lawn with the garden hose. Our coffee pot was precariously balanced on a chair in the dining room, and the refrigerator, displaced next to the couch, was full of pizza boxes and bottled water.

For reasons I truly cannot comprehend now, in the midst of the work, we had an absolutely massive garage sale. We needed to do it before putting our house on the market, and I was so antsy to move on, literally and figuratively, that I failed to think through how the construction and the garage sale would actually work, right at the same time.

I'm a really bad candidate for a garage sale, because I like giving things away more than I like selling them, and because I lose interest in the whole enterprise rather quickly. I like tagging things for a while, and then I wander away. I sit at the cash table for a while, and then I get really hungry and order pizza for all of us at ten in the morning, spending all our morning's proceeds.

At this particular sale, I got a little carried away and gave our only TV to my sister-in-law, because we planned on getting a new one when we moved. Aaron asked me later why I didn't just say we'd give it to her when we actually moved, why I practically put it in her car for her. I don't really know why, except that something came over me during the sale. I would have sold my feet for a good offer. I was drunk on the prospect of clean closets and psychic freedom and that smooth little stack of bills in the cashbox, and it made me give away our TV. And a fair amount of other things we actually should have kept. I also sold a table but, inexplicably, kept the chairs, sold an antique bed frame but forgot to include most of the pieces, and sneaked odd little extra items into people's bags every so often, just so I'd have a little less cleanup later.

Every night after Henry went to sleep, Aaron and I collapsed onto the couch and watched bad movies and overate comfort foods. We'd settle into the brown chair, the one that fits us just perfectly, and I'd drink red wine and eat superhuman amounts of hummus or goat cheese or cold pizza. We stared at the TV, until, of course, I gave it away. We ate mindlessly, trying to avoid everything: the move, the mess of remodeling, the good parts and the hard parts of leaving a place we'd grown to love, the anxiety that the next place would not make all our dreams come true, and the sinking realization that we still believed in the concept of all our dreams coming true, despite current observable reality.

We said, abstractly, that we wanted to arrive in Chicago sharp and healthy and focused, ready to connect and build a new way of living. At the rate we were going, however, we'd arrive in Chicago totally off our rockers, cranky and more caffeine-addicted than ever, wild-eyed and bloated. And since that's just about the way we arrived in Grand Rapids six years ago, we realized we were in great danger, that our past was becoming our future, and that something had to change.

It felt like all of life was in someone else's hands—the church in Chicago had a final decision to make about Aaron's pending job, an imaginary buyer had a house to fall in love with, but there was so little we could do. And so we did nothing. We ate and watched reruns on our laptops and developed an addiction to the news coverage of the presidential election, scouring cnn .com for article after article as a way of distracting ourselves.

And then all at once, Aaron said he wanted—or rather needed—to fast, the spiritual discipline of going without food for a specific amount of time as a way of trusting God's provision and creating silence and space for prayer. He said he needed to do something to honor God's role in all this and to prepare himself as best he could for a new future. I said I'd join him, as did our friends Steve and Sarah, whose lives were disturbingly similar to ours during that season—baby boy, house for sale, waiting for decisions that would change everything but that hadn't yet been made. We decided together to have nothing but juice or broth for one week, and to pray in the morning and the evening, all at the same time, wherever we were, whatever we were doing.

It felt significant to me that one year earlier I was fasting in preparation for the release of my first book. I fasted then for twenty days, not because the number was significant, but because the number of days between the day on which I was desperate enough to begin the fast and the day of the first release party happened to be twenty. Lest you think that I am a frequent fast-er, and kind of a show-off, these are the only two fasts of any length I've ever done. And lest you think I'm showing a new, entirely surprising superspiritual side, fasting, the way I understand it, is more about desperation than anything else. Some people are connected enough with God on a day-to-day basis to go without fasting. Some people weather major life changes with aplomb and Pilates and vegetables, just like how they live the rest of their orderly, lovely lives. I, however, was feeling totally untethered to God or anything else and wanted to find a way to connect once again to the things that matter to me. Fasting was a move of desperation.

And so on a Saturday morning we began, and by about 10 a.m., we were cranky. We went to the Eastown street fair, crowded with popcorn and elephant ears and coffee and pastries. Possibly a poor choice. The fast was embarrassingly hard for the first few days. We were vaguely angry about everything and tried to alternately blame each other and find loopholes. But at the same time we were also surprisingly clearheaded. I felt like I could see things I didn't usually see, like my mind and spirit were wiped clean and working well for the first time in what seemed like forever. I felt able and bright-minded, and both those things were very unusual for me in that season. I slept like a rock and woke up easily. And when I prayed, I found my prayers to be full of peace, expectation, confidence. I didn't feel the same panic and anxiety that had been marking my days previously. I felt hungry but clean and strong.

During the fast, we found a house in Chicago. I immediately had a feeling about it. This is the one, I thought. It felt significant and right that after so many months of wondering, we would find our new home during the fast, and it has proven to be just the right home for us in this season. I made progress on many of the things I'd been dragging my feet on for weeks. At night, with no option to eat and no TV to watch, Aaron and I settled into opposite sides of the couch, alternately reading and talking, and then went to bed early and slept well.

I found the rhythm of set prayer times to be kind of an undergirding to my day. In some ways it was a week of complaining and hunger and silence, but in other ways, it was a grounding, exciting week, opening us to a better way of living. As always, when I do something that people have been doing for thousands of years, like reading the Bible or fasting or set prayer times, at first I think I've stumbled upon something very significant, and that I should try to tell a lot of people about this new, wonderful thing.

And then just a second later, I realize that there's nothing new about it, and that the reason people have been doing it for thousands of years is because it matters, because it does something inside of the people who do it. It's not a new practice or the next big idea. It's an enduring way of living that has been shaping and reshaping people for years. When I fasted and prayed on a set rhythm, I felt like I was a part of something old and durable. I felt humble, one more set of footprints on a dusty well-worn path, discovering something new that's not new at all, and I was thankful.

seven

THINGS I DON'T DO

A few years ago, at the very end of my frantic twenties, I was working more than full-time, all the while pricked with invisible needles of dissatisfaction, waking up in the night longing to write, buzzing through the days on coffee and adrenaline, wearing clothes that should have been taken to the dry cleaner six wearings ago. I was trying to think about becoming a mother. I knew it would change everything, but I couldn't picture it, because no one ever can. I couldn't see a way through to any other way of living, but I knew that there must be one. I saw women who were older than me, who did work they believed in and parented well, and, most surprisingly, didn't seem nearly as frantic and chronically unkempt. I wanted what they had, and I had no idea how to get it.

I love the illusion of being able to do it all, and I'm fascinated with people who seem to do that, who have challenging careers and beautiful homes and vibrant minds and well-tended abs. Throw in polite children and a garden, and I'm coming over for lessons.

Out to lunch one day with my friend Denise, I asked her about it. Denise is a mother of four, and a grandmother, and she works and writes and travels and cooks, and—most important to me at that time—she seems settled in some fundamental way. There's something she knows about herself that I didn't yet know about myself, certainly.

We were at the Blue Water Grill, on a beautiful lake, unless you're from Grand Rapids, apparently, because then you know that it used to be a quarry, and to them it's sort of like having lunch crater-side. But it's beautiful to me, having only known it as a lake. We ate pesto pizza and spinach salad with red onion slivers and poppyseed dressing, and long after the food was cleared, we drank iced tea and watched the water.

And this is what Denise told me: she said it's not hard to decide what you want your life to be about. What's hard, she said, is figuring out what you're willing to give up in order to do the things you really care about. Her words from that day have been rattling around inside me for years now, twisting around, whispering, taking shape. Since that time we've worked together, traveled together, cried together, but when I think of her, I will always think of that day, and the wind on the fake lake, and the clarity and weight of those words.

I'm a list-keeper. I always, always have a to-do list, and it ranges from the mundane: go to the dry cleaner, go to the post office, buy batteries; to the far-reaching: stop eating Henry's leftover Dino Bites, get over yourself, forgive nasty reviewer, wear more jewelry.

At one point, I kept adding to the list, more and more

items, more and more sweeping in their scope, until I added this line: DO EVERYTHING BETTER. It was, at the time, a pretty appropriate way to capture how I felt about my life and myself fairly often. It also explains why I tended to get so tired I'd cry without knowing why, why my life sometimes felt like I was running on a hamster wheel, and why I searched the faces of calmer, more grounded women for a secret they all knew that I didn't. This is how I got to that fragmented, brittle, lonely place: DO EVERYTHING BETTER.

Each of the three words has a particular flavor of poison all its own. *Do:* we know better than *do*, of course. We know that words like "be," and "become," and "try" are a little less crushing and cruel, spiritually and psychologically, a little friendlier to the soul. But when we're alone sometimes and the list is getting the best of us, we abandon all those sweet ideas, and we go straight to *do*, because *do* is power, push, aggression, plain old sweat equity. It's not pretty, but we know that *do* gets the job done.

Everything is just a killer. *Everything* is the heart of the conversation for me, my drug of choice. Sure, I can host that party. Of course, I can bring that meal. Yes, I'd love to write that article. Yes, to *everything*.

This winter, I got the kind of tired that you can't recover from, almost like something gets altered on a cellular level, and you begin to fantasize about what it would be like to just not be tired anymore. You don't fantasize about money or men or the Italian Riviera. All you daydream about is not feeling exhausted, about neck muscles that don't throb, about a mind that isn't fogged every single day. I was talking to my husband about it in the car one night. I was complaining about being tired, but also bringing up the fact that lots of women travel and work and have kids. Everybody has a house to clean. Why can't I pull it together?

He said, gently, ostensibly helpfully, something along the lines of "you know, honey, just because some other people can do all that, it doesn't mean that you can or have to. Maybe it's too much for you."

One tiny, almost imperceptible beat of silence. And then I yelled, viscerally, from the depths of my soul, as though possessed, "I'M NOT WEAK!"

As soon as the words came out, we looked at each other in alarm. It seemed, perhaps, we'd hit upon the heart of something. One of my core fears is that someone would think I can't handle as much as the next person. It's fundamental to my understanding of myself for me to be the strong one, the capable one, the busy one, the one who can bail you out, not make a fuss, bring a meal, add a few more things to the list. For me, *everything* becomes a lifestyle. *Everything* is an addiction.

And then *better. Better* is a seductress. It's so delicious to run after *better, better, better. Better* is what keeps some women decorating and redecorating the same house for years on end, because by the time you get the last detail of the finished basement home theater just right, your countertops are just ever so slightly outdated, and so you start again. *Better* is what makes us go to a spinning class—or maybe two, or maybe three today, just for good measure. *Better* is what makes us get "just a little work done," after the last baby, you know, or just to look a little bit fresher and more well-rested. *Better* is a force.

The three together, DO EVERYTHING BETTER, are a supercharged triple threat, capturing in three words the mania of modern life, the antispirit, antispiritual, soul-shriveling garbage that infects and compromises our lives. And I'm the one who wrote those words on my very own to-do list. I'm in a lot of trouble with my own self for that, because the "do everything better" way of living brought me to a terrible place: tired, angry, brittle, afraid, hollow. And Denise's words keep ringing in my ears, a song I had heard in the distance, like steel drums across the water, a song I want desperately to hear again.

She was right. Deciding what I wanted wasn't that hard. But deciding what I'm willing to give up for those things is like yoga for your superego, stretching and pushing and ultimately healing that nasty little person inside of you who exists only for what people think.

Things I Do:

Above all else, I try to keep my faith in Christ at the very center of my life, the heart and source of everything. I trust God's voice as my guide and Christ as my comforter. I pray, I practice confession and forgiveness, and I seek to see the world through the eyes of its Creator, believing everything can be redeemed. I'm a part of my church community, volunteering on its behalf, and working to make a better city and a better world because of our church community.

I do everything I can to make my marriage a deeply connected partnership. I work hard at being a good partner to Aaron, to walk with him and hear him and learn with him.

I give the best of my day to raise my son, and I dream about being a mother to more children someday. For the record, though, I did not and do not do very many of those super-achiever-mom things, like making baby food from scratch. I think the baby food people are doing a very nice job making baby food, and I bought it at Target.

I work hard to become a better writer with each page. I want to tell the truth as best I can, to tell the story of God and who he is and what he does, both through the way I write and the way I live. I write and read, in airports and hotel rooms and coffee shops and in the little blue room in our house. I read novels and essays and magazines and cookbooks and the Bible, and I couldn't live well without those things.

I live in daily, honest, intimate community with a small group of people. I give my time and energy and prayer to my immediate family and close friends. To a slightly wider circle of people, I give them my love and friendship through intermittent emails and very occasional visits.

Our home is a place of celebration and comfort for people we love, so I cook and entertain a lot, because it makes me feel alive and happy, the perfect counterpoint to the other part of my life—the lonely, typing part. It seems, I know, like one of the things that should be the first to go, along with novels, maybe, but I can't live well without gathering people around our table. It gives me energy and creativity and spark, so it stays.

And then there are, of course, a few other things I do, just for being a person in America who does not have a personal assistant and is not, say, the president. This list includes, but is not limited to: trips to the DMV, laundry folding, diaper buying, and occasional flossing. Even if I did have a personal assistant, I would stipulate that I still do my own flossing, because I'm just that grounded.

So those are the things I do, things I believe in or feel called to, or just things that fall within my area of responsibility on the planetary chore list. But the more important list is the other one: the list of things I don't do. I come back to it regularly, adding to it. The first list was easy. And then came the hard part. What am I willing to *not* do in order to do these things I believe in? Silence. Blank paper. More silence. Finally, a few things came to mind.

Things I Don't Do:

I don't garden. Our landscaping in Grand Rapids was so bad that Becky, our neighbor, came over of her own accord and dug out all our beds, partially because she's a wonderful person and partially, I'm sure, because five years of driving past the wreckage of our front yard very nearly drove her to the brink of insanity. I've been feeling like sort of a loser because I don't garden. I have friends who garden, and they talk a lot about the spiritual implications of new life springing from the earth, the deep communion with God that they experience as they lovingly tend to their herbs and flowers. But I'm going to have to miss out on all that, because, at least for now, no gardening.

I don't do major home improvement projects or scour flea markets and antique shops for the perfect home accessories. No expectation for perfect housekeeping, either—I try for clean countertops and no horrible smells, but beyond that, it's pretty rough. At our house, "home improvement" involves clearing off the coffee table every few days and loading and unloading the dishwasher.

I don't always change my clothes just because I'm leaving the house. I wear yoga pants 99 percent of the time, and I pretend that other people don't notice that I'm wearing my pajamas in public.

I don't make our bed in the morning, standing firm on the adolescent belief that there's no sense in doing something you're just going to undo at the end of the day.

I don't bake. I don't like to bake, because there's too much math and science involved. I purchase cakes from the bakery or serve chocolates and fruit. I know baking is such a mom thing to do, and that possibly my son would be happier if the aroma of freshly baked bread or cookies woke him from his naptime slumber. But at least for now, no baking, during naptime or any other time.

Scrapbooking and photo album making are both on the list, although I do take a lot of pictures of my kid with my phone.

I only blow-dry my hair on special occasions, and my fingernails haven't been painted since the nineties. There's only so much time.

I don't spend time with people who routinely make me feel like less than I am, or who spend most of their time talking about what's wrong with everyone else and what's wrong with the world, or who really like to talk about other people's money.

It's brutal, making the list of Things I Don't Do, especially for someone like me, who refuses most of the time to acknowledge that there is, in fact, a limit to her personal ability to get things done. But I've discovered that the list sets me free. I have it written in black and white, sitting on my desk, and when I'm tempted to go rogue and bake muffins because all the other moms do, I come back to both lists, and I remind myself about the important things: that time is finite, as is energy. And that one day I'll stand before God and account for what I did with my life. There is work that is only mine to do: a child that is ours to raise, stories that are mine to tell, friends that are mine to walk with. The grandest seduction of all is the myth that DOING EVERYTHING BETTER gets us where we want to be. It gets us somewhere, certainly, but not anywhere worth being.

eight

ALAMEDA

Henry and I flew to visit Kirsten and her baby Cash at their house in Alameda, across the bay from San Francisco. Her husband took their older son to Legoland for the weekend, and Sara flew in from Boston, and Monica drove over the mountain from Reno with her newborn son Tate. If you don't have a calculator in front of you, that's three baby boys under eight months, and four college girlfriends in a two-bedroom house for three days. It was just amazing.

Some of the magic of the weekend, for me, was Alameda itself. I have a thing for California, possibly because the four years I lived there during college were the wildest and most disorienting years, punctuated by some of the sweetest moments in all my life. Possibly because California, both in its geography and its personality, is so many worlds away from the Midwest that just being there makes the world feel bigger. I love California for its otherness, for its profound non-Midwest-ness.

I love the smell of eucalyptus and salt and the attitude and the stucco houses and the ubiquitous tiny Toyota pickups. There's an order to the Midwest: flat land, predictable seasons, apples and cherries and white Christmases, a sense of tradition and stability. But California to me is entirely other, and the fact that Kirsten has a lemon tree right in her backyard never fails to delight me. A lemon tree!

Because Henry was still on Michigan time, Kirsten went above and beyond as the hostess of the century and woke up with us hours before sunrise. We put Henry and Cash in their strollers between four-thirty and five each morning and walked with them in the cool morning air along the beach, and when the coffee shop finally opened at six a.m., we rolled in our little brigade and drank lattes and ate giant morning glory muffins. We talked about babies and college and marriage and fitting into your pre-baby pants. We decided that that last one is overrated for the time being, and Kirsten stopped her stroller on the sidewalk at one point, for emphasis, and made me promise to pack up all my too-small pre-baby clothes and put them away somewhere where they couldn't taunt me every day. I promised, and then we kept rolling.

The whole weekend, we never went anywhere in the car, because we couldn't get all of us and all the car seats in one car, so we walked everywhere with our strollers, to get ice cream and coffee and, hands down, the best Chinese takeout I've ever had. One afternoon Kirsten roasted a chicken and some kale—crispy, almost nutty—and we sat on a blanket in the backyard in the sun, letting the boys roll around, telling the same college stories we've all told and all heard five hundred times. We slept in different places every night, depending on whose baby was sleeping when and where, and we just kept rotating from the kitchen to the sunny backyard to the front porch to the fluffy rug in the living room, feeding babies and telling stories.

We laid on the blanket under the lemon tree drinking Sancerre while the babies napped, and in those moments I realized why this kind of time together matters so much: because there are things you can't know, and questions you can't ask, and memories you can't recover via email and voicemail. It was about the being there, about being there to really see what's exactly the same and what's totally different about each one of us.

It's possible for motherhood, especially new motherhood, to be so entirely isolating. You live in the rarified world of your house with a tiny darling who doesn't talk, and you stumble through the days, one blending into the next, in yoga pants smeared with diaper cream, nursing and rocking, nursing and rocking. Your world changes utterly, but your friends' lives don't, necessarily. They love your new little one, but they either have older children and remember this season well, and are a little glad they're finished with it, or they don't have their own children and can't imagine it. In any case, you're the only one in the newborn fog. But for a weekend in Alameda, we weren't alone at all.

Because we had the time, because we could let conversations wind and unwind, because we could start them at dawn and pick them up again in the afternoon and add a few more thoughts in the evening, we circled down to the places you never get to when you just see one another at weddings, giving out funny sound bytes over bites of cake.

In the same way that we helped each other figure out how to get the babies to sleep, and all threw in our opinions about a good marinade for skirt steak, we offered one another our stories and bits of advice, the scraps of wisdom and experience we've gathered up around ourselves along the way. We're not therapists or child development experts, but we're giving everything we can to our families, and really, the challenges are pretty similar. The solutions are, too: we found that almost every one of the rough spots we discussed under the trees could use an extra round of listening, a liberal dose of forgiveness, and a solid effort at empathy.

We talked, of course, a lot about parenting. A large part of parenting comes down to observing your actual little person, and shuffling through acres of advice to select the piece that meets your little one's need just perfectly. It all comes down to close observation, willingness to take advice, ability to try something new when all the old things have stopped working.

When we'd exhausted the topic of parenting, we moved on to creativity, work, poetry, and organic farming. We recommended books to one another, long lists, knowing well enough by now what each of us prefers to read, and we listened to Brandi Carlile and Jenny Lewis while we fed our boys yogurt and peas. We talked about music, the environment, what we've learned about money, and what our mutual college friends are doing with their lives. Because it's the thing that gathered us together in the first place, we talked a lot about writing. We met in college, all English majors. And now we are all writers in various capacities, trying to find the space and freedom to write with full-time jobs or newborns or paralyzing fear.

There were more questions than answers that weekend.

What do you do once you've written a dissertation? How do you walk away from a decade of work, even if you don't necessarily love it? How do work and babies and dreams and marriages and mortgages fit together in one life, and if something has to give, what gives?

I still don't know the answers to a lot of those questions, but I know that right in this moment, as I sit at my kitchen table looking out at a decidedly Midwestern landscape, the smell of lemons and salty sea air come right back to me in an instant, and I remember those days, and I remember that the answers aren't necessarily as important as the questions and the company, and that if we do find answers, we'll find them together.

If you're lucky enough to have your Monica and your Sara and your Kirsten all right in your very own town, I hope you soak it up, and that you lie around in each other's backyards every Saturday afternoon or stay up late on one another's porches three nights a week. But if you're like me, and if those faces are far away, get a weekend on the calendar and get there.

Share your life with the people you love, even if it means saving up for a ticket and going without a few things for a while to make it work. There are enough long lonely days of the same old thing, and if you let enough years pass, and if you let the routine steamroll your life, you'll wake up one day, isolated and weary, and wonder what happened to all those old friends. You'll wonder why all you share is Christmas cards, and why life feels lonely and bone-dry. We were made to live connected and close, as close as we all were for those few days in Alameda, holding one another's babies, taking turns stirring whatever's on the stove.

So walk across the street, or drive across town, or fly across the country, but don't let really intimate loving friendships become the last item on a long to-do list. Good friendships are like breakfast. You think you're too busy to eat breakfast, but then you find yourself exhausted and cranky halfway through the day, and discover that your attempt to save time totally backfired. In the same way, you can try to go it alone because you don't have time or because your house is too messy to have people over, or because making new friends is like the very worst parts of dating. But halfway through a hard day or a hard week, you'll realize in a flash that you're breathtakingly lonely, and that the Christmas cards aren't much company. Get up, make a phone call, buy a cheap ticket, open your front door.

Because there really is nothing like good friends, like the sounds of their laughter and the tones of their voices and the things they teach us in the quietest, smallest moments.

nine

WHAT WE LEFT IN SOUTH BEND

On a cloudy Sunday, Aaron and I went to South Bend. I had a TV interview there early on Monday morning, so we drove in the night before and had dinner with our friend Jason, who has two Golden Retrievers with whom Henry developed a deep love/fear relationship. He so badly wanted to touch them and be near them but gripped our hands tightly as he inched up to them and clung to us like a starfish when they tried to lick him.

When we got to the hotel and got Henry to sleep, I developed a dramatic, violent stomach flu. I had felt it coming on for a few days, and I was up all night. The interview was a near disaster, because I kept forgetting what I was talking about, too busy looking for garbage cans and exits.

The most important thing that happened in South Bend,

though, had nothing to do with the interview. Before Jason's house, before the vomiting, before the interview, Aaron and I struck an important agreement. We decided to leave a tangled-up mess of six months of *you-did, you-should-have, you-said* right there in South Bend. We had been injuring one another for months, in the name of honest discussion, beating the same dead horses, as they say, to dust. We were so deeply tired of fighting the same fight so many times, of apologizing for the same things, accusing one another of the same things, that we decided there was nothing to do but leave those fights in South Bend. From then on, we were free to fight about anything we wanted, but not if it was something we left in South Bend, because we left it there forever, and it could not be resurrected. We decided that there had to be a statute of limitations, and that it had to be invoked right then in South Bend, or we'd be stuck indefinitely.

It was the middle of such a tricky, hard season in our lives, one with so much loss and so many questions. We knew that we needed our marriage to be a healing and helping force in the midst of it, a harbor in the storm. We knew that, but at the same time we couldn't figure out how to actually do that. We retreated, accused, let our fear loom larger than our ability to forgive. We added to the weight of the season, piled the fear and loneliness on one another's shoulders instead of offering to carry a burden for the other.

We were so tired and disoriented by the direction our lives had taken that we both wanted to take it out on someone else a little bit. For a while, we behaved poorly, over and over, and then for a while after that, we spent hours rehashing just how poorly the other one had behaved, as though we hadn't both been present for every single conversation: "But you did, that one time, say *this!*" "I still remember how much it hurt when you did *that!*" Over and over. It was like being on a highway with no exits, feeling the mounting pressure that you must find another road but don't know how. With every passing mile, you become both more despairing and more focused, frantic with fear and bad scenarios.

Aaron and I are finding that marriage, and maybe all relationships, are built on the past. That's a good thing, when the past involves honeymoons and great dates and moments of sweetness and partnership. But what are we left with when, increasingly, the past also contains the moments when we hurt each other, the times we stopped listening, the needs we saw and didn't meet, the conversations we walked away from?

We were stuck, and it felt like you could have subbed in a prerecorded version of the same old fight we'd had a thousand times. We kept thinking that if we talked about it one more time, we would break through to something, but that wasn't happening. Instead of breaking through, we were just breaking apart, bit by bit, blow by blow, you-should-have by you-should-have. It was a conversation that centered itself entirely in the past, and it kept us there, unable to move into a new future, forced to re-create a future that was a terrible mirror of a past we just couldn't shake.

We had forgiven one another before, many times, but every time the stress ratcheted up a few notches, all of a sudden our memories became practically photographic. My husband can't remember the names of people we see on a regular basis, and all of a sudden he could remember every single time I pushed too hard, every time I rolled my eyes, figuratively and, I'm sorry to admit, literally. We had developed Rain Man-like abilities to recall even the smallest of offenses, to resurrect them over and over and insert them into present conversation as though they had just happened earlier that day. We had forgiven, as well as we knew how. But it turned out we didn't know how to do it well enough, and our marriage was creaking and groaning under the weight of all the things we had, ostensibly, forgiven, but certainly not forgotten.

But in South Bend, we dropped it all—the accusations, the things we should have done and didn't do and couldn't manage and couldn't be for one another—and we decided to start over. One more apology from either one of us wasn't going to be a magic wand, wiping it all away. There was nothing left to be said, on either side. We just had to put it down and walk away from it, because we both knew that we were in danger of becoming one of those couples whose future is always overshadowed by their past, who remembers the offenses more clearly than anything else. We were in love, and we shared a million things between us, not the least of which was a child who was almost old enough to understand these terrible circular conversations. Our lives were knitted together with memories and kindnesses and shared visions for life and marriage. We were connected by more than these resentments, but it was becoming harder and harder to believe that. We had to do something, and fast.

If God removes our sin as far as the East is from the West, then for Aaron and me to leave our offenses in South Bend is a good start, I think. The absence of all the things we left there has created space for new things, good things, new patterns to be built, new moments of warmth and connectedness.

We're starting to be able to really hear one another again, and listen again, and carry each other, because our arms aren't so full of all the things we've been carrying for months.

So I'm sorry to you, South Bend, but on your streets and sidewalks, two people left a lot of fear and disappointment and accusation and despair, and we're not coming back for them anytime soon. It's nothing personal, of course, just the place we happened to be when our arms got too tired, finally, to keep carrying the same old tangled-up mess.

ten

FEEDING AND BEING FED

I'm a big believer in for-no-reason parties—last-minute parties, where the house is less than squeaky clean, where the guest list is "whoever could come with three days' notice," and the menu is "whatever I could think of and whatever goes with feta or chutney."

There's something about seeing your house filled with people you love, something about feeding people, especially on days when it seems like you can't make a dent in any of the larger, more theoretical challenges in life.

I don't know where we'll be in five years or how exactly we'll pay the mortgage the next few months or when we'll have another child, but I do know how to make dinner, and to see the people I care about gobble it up makes me feel like something is right, even when it seems like nothing is.

There's something so healing about those quiet moments at the table, when everyone's mouth—or mind or heart—is full, when you feel connected and nourished and content, even if it's just for a split second.

In February, my friend Kelly and I decided to have a party because we both felt that life was sort of blank during that season: snowy and dim and the bad kind of quiet—the kind when you think everyone you know might be at a party you weren't invited to. Kelly's younger than I am, and single, and I thought that if even she was feeling isolated, things were indeed dire, because I assume she's partying like a rock star seven nights a week. My dear friend Ruth talked about a similar sense of isolation, and she's one of those women whose refrigerator door is filled with overlapping invitations to fundraisers and events. She's on committees and boards and goes to *galas*. If she was feeling lonely, things were bleaker, certainly, than I had previously imagined.

We decided to take matters into our own hands, to create a space that felt rich and well-populated in the midst of those blank days. I proposed Italian food—warm, heavily flavored, comforting, sprawled out over a table, unfussy. And the guest list was similar, a rich and varied group of women, some who knew one another and many who didn't. In some calendar miracle, almost everyone could come. There were twelve in total: a few women from our book club, some of Kelly's close friends, and my oldest Grand Rapids friends. Emily came after work, and even Stefany came. Stefany is in the category of people I really, really like and somehow never see, so I was thrilled that she was free.

I intended to make the perfect dinner party playlist, but I

had been listening to the *Once* soundtrack and couldn't bear to stop, so a few times at the table, we found ourselves all listening for the best moments, cocking our ears, trying not to sing out loud.

Kelly and I asked everyone to bring part of the meal. We also asked them to bring some money, whatever amount felt right to them, for the church in our neighborhood that feeds people from a truck a few times a month. I put my little red tomato pot next to the wine and glasses in the living room, and at the end of the night it was full. It felt right to think about other people's hunger as we were thinking about our own—hunger for food and for friendship, for nourishment of many kinds.

Melissa from my book club made fantastic Italian hummus, and Kelly and Lacey brought bread and cheese and wine. We caught up in the living room, piling up coats in the foyer, unwrapping platters in the kitchen. And when it was time to eat, the table was gorgeous and full—pastas and risotto and salads and roasted asparagus with garlic aioli. We told stories and passed bowls and laughed at Julie's punch lines. Every time I left the room to get something in the kitchen, there was a scandalous whoop of laughter from her end of the table, and a guilty Cheshire cat smile on her face every time I returned.

After dinner, we sat around the coffee table eating Stefany's flourless chocolate cake with crème anglaise and champagne, lots of little clusters of conversations, occasional bubbles of laughter in the dim light of the living room. We washed the dishes together, packing up pastas and cheeses, wiping platters, bringing bottles out to the recycling bin.

I stayed up late, long after they all left, letting the candles burn down, trying to remember each moment, exactly how the table looked and how each bite tasted. I felt nourished on an impossibly deep level, thankful and full and proud and humbled all in the same moment. It felt to me like we'd been a part of something important, something larger than a meal, like we'd managed to thaw the ice just for an evening, like we had traversed bridges normally impassable. Even the next morning, Aaron kept remarking that I seemed so unusually buoyant. It may have been that I had Stefany's chocolate cake for both breakfast and lunch, but in any case, I fairly glided through the day, bouncing on the bright feelings of the night before as I placed the wineglasses back into the hutch and counted out the money from my red pot, sealing it into an envelope for my neighbor, the pastor of the food truck church.

Sometimes the most spiritual things we do are the most physical, the most tactile. Feeding people is one of those things, whether we're helping to feed hungry people, or feeding the hunger in each one of us on these dark and heavy winter nights.

eleven

SEA DREAMING

After years of dreaming about it and months of talking about it, my brother, Todd, and our dear friend Joe officially decided to sail around the world, to leave their jobs and homes, to sell guitars and motorcycles and fancy bachelor TVs and take a once-in-a-lifetime trip. They bought a boat last June and worked on it all summer in the harbor in South Haven.

On the evening of Henry's first birthday, our family and friends had a late dinner, and Todd and Joe still had work to do on the boat before leaving at dawn. My mom went to Walmart in the middle of the night, even though she'd been there twice during the day already, because she kept thinking of one more thing to pack into one more drawer—cans of food, cleaning supplies, extra everything.

Early the next morning, we stood on the dock while Todd and Joe silently stowed the last few items, did the last few chores. We drank coffee in the dark and took turns snuggling

Henry in his footie pajamas. We stood in a circle and prayed for safety and wisdom and kind seas.

Our family rule is that we never pray for adventure, especially when it's about a boat. On one family vacation twenty years ago, a guest asked for adventure as she prayed before breakfast, and then we sailed straight into a tropical depression, complete with swirling winds, lightning, and an unrelenting downpour. We never saw the sun again that trip, and now we never, ever pray for adventure.

As the sun rose, we followed Todd and Joe down the channel in dinghies, like a floating parade, waving and taking pictures and wiping tears, and then they were gone. They sailed north through the Great Lakes, down the Hudson River, down the east coast, to the Bahamas, Florida, the Caribbean, and then the Panama Canal and the Galapagos. They spent twenty days out of sight of land, and then arrived in the Marquesas, then Tahiti, then the Cook Islands.

Aaron and I went to visit them, and when we met them in Fiji, they'd been aboard for eight months. We'd received brief satellite email updates from them almost every day—highlights, wind speed and direction, miles traveled—and exchanged more lengthy emails when they were at port, able to post pictures and longer updates.

A trip to Fiji wasn't necessarily in the plans or in the budget, but it was one of those opportunities you just don't miss. My parents felt strongly about it and gave us their frequent flyer miles for the tickets. We planned the trip relatively last minute and scheduled it in between several work trips, so it sneaked up on us. All of a sudden, it seemed, we were throwing our swimsuits and fins in a bag, leaving for, of all places, Fiji. In our flurry, Aaron left our credit card at O'Hare while buying a neck pillow and Godiva chocolates, and when we got to LAX, we learned via text from a friend back in Grand Rapids that our kitchen and basement had flooded. The middle of the night in the international terminal became a blur of insurance calls, calls to the credit card company, hastily eaten Mexican food, and a funny bout of vomiting. It could have been the Mexican food. Or it could have been the fact that water was flowing freely from our kitchen to our basement, and we were two thousand miles away and about to get even farther.

We got on the plane anyway and arrived in Fiji at five in the morning, without our bags, which, at that point, seemed fitting. We bought outrageously expensive coffees and cashews to bolster our spirits, and took a cab to the marina.

And then when we arrived, as you always hope it will on faraway trips, time stopped. We were in another world. We still texted back and forth with Lindsay about whether or not the kitchen floor should be ripped out. We still got daily updates about what Henry was doing with Nana and Papa. But we were across both the equator and the International Date Line. We were in another world entirely.

Fiji is all the things you imagine it is: lush green mountains rising up out of navy seas, thatched-roof huts, crescent beaches lined with palms. It is beyond beautiful, a postcard everywhere you look. We arrived in the rainy season, which means luscious purple clouds roll in like freight trains, rain falls in sheets, and then the clouds rise and retreat an hour later, the sky clean and sparkling.

Living on a sailboat is a funny mix of luxury and camping. The stars are impossibly bright and the sound of the wind in the rigging never gets old, but you do shower with your swimsuit on standing on the back deck of the boat, and dinner is made by opening several different cans—meats, vegetables, possibly peaches or mandarin oranges for dessert.

We sailed and snorkeled and visited islands. The boys always wanted to know what was under the water—sharks, sea snakes, reefs, but I wanted to know what was ashore—villages and beach bars and children selling shells and necklaces, the strands hung from low palm branches.

The combination of being so far away and of living according to such an entirely different rhythm cut through convention and polite conversation and made it possible to talk about the things that usually lie several levels down. We had so much time, as the boat sliced through the water, as the sun rose over a green mountain, burning through fog and silence, as roosters crowed in villages, and fires were lit on beaches in the soft morning light. We were silent a lot, reading and writing, living in our own worlds, especially in the mornings. But as the sun rose, we told stories and asked questions and lived in the luxury of having more than enough time to talk about every single thing.

The month before we visited, Joe proposed to his girlfriend Emily who was visiting him in Tahiti. He went to a pearl farm before she arrived and chose a perfect black pearl set in white gold, and he asked her to be his wife as the sun set over the green islands. I drove him nuts wanting to hear every detail, and he dreamed with us about what life would be like when he got back, about their wedding, their home, the life waiting for him in Grand Rapids.

Joe is a wanderer. He always wants to be somewhere else, to be somewhere more exciting. And now in the middle of the South Pacific, all he wants is Grand Rapids, and Emily, and the new life they'll have together. Sometimes we have to leave home in order to find out what we left there, and why it matters so much.

One night, at a tiny restaurant on the Blue Lagoon— seriously, the actual Blue Lagoon, of Brooke Shields fame— between bites of lobster ravioli and spicy grilled lamb, we talked about the things we want to do in our lives. The four of us have spent thousands of hours together, so many summers and vacations, boating and joking and talking about nothing. But this is a funny season in all four of our lives, one with more questions than answers, when it's kind of all open, waiting to be re-created, each on the cusp of something, but we don't know what. So we talked about how we think God made each of us, what we're good at, what we're not, what we might do, what we never will.

Sometimes we get so tangled up in our own perceptions of ourselves, what we think we're good at and what we're not, that we lose perspective, seeing only our failures and bad habits. I can give you a top ten list of why it's hard to work with me or crazy-making to live with me, and especially in difficult seasons, it's almost impossible to remember that feeling of being great at something, or the feeling of being proud of yourself.

We reminded one another that night, and we dreamed on behalf of one another. We pushed and encouraged and let the silences open wide every once in a while, to let things sink in and settle. Left to our own devices, we sometimes choose the most locked up, dark versions of the story, but what a good friend does is turn on the lights, open the window, and remind us that there are a whole lot of ways to tell the same story.

The conversation felt as fresh and possible as the wind blowing in off the lagoon. That's why travel is so important, among other reasons: to get far enough away from our everyday lives to see those lives with new clarity. When you're literally on the other side of the world, when you're under the silent sea, watching a bright, silent world of fish and coral, when you're staring up at a sky so bright and dense with stars it makes you gasp, it's in those moments that you begin to see the fullness of your life, the possibility that still prevails, that always prevails.

You certainly don't have to be on the other side of the world, but you do have to get out of those same four walls you're always staring at. Drive to the city, or to the country, or to a lake whose shores are totally unfamiliar to you. Listen for the new rhythms and sounds, and watch your life refract and shift against a new backdrop. You'll see things you didn't know were there, and recognize selves long hidden. Sometimes a totally new sense of possibility is found practically in your own backyard, viewed for the first time from an entirely new vantage point.

That night we talked and talked, after tables emptied one by one, in the flickering light from the torches. We dreamed, for ourselves and for one another. You could do that! You were made for this! I've always dreamed of that!

I stop dreaming sometimes, because I'm afraid of what it would take to change my life. I stop dreaming because I'm afraid of the chaos that a dream might bring, afraid of what a new dream will require of me. I practice being fine, and I tell myself that things are all right, just as they are. They are all right, of course.

But that night, with my husband and my brother and my

dear friend, I dreamed. And it could have been the beauty of the moon on the water, or it could have been the freshness of the sea air, but when I returned home, I felt new, and that the world was bright and new, and I heard God's voice whispering to me everywhere I went. It could have been anything, but I think it was the dreaming.

twelve

GRACE IS NEW MATH

I've decided that this is going to be the year of grace in my life. For every Christian, every year, of course, is the year of grace. But I think the nature of being a Christian—or, really, the nature of learning anything over a lifetime—is that sometimes you wake up and realize that somehow you're missing an essential part of your education, and that now is the time to start learning and relearning. These things go in waves, it seems.

For example, it seems to me that for chefs and food writers, it's all about smoking your own bacon this year. That sounds delicious. It's not a brand new idea. People have been doing it for ages, but it's definitely topping the trend lists this year. In the same way, grace isn't a new idea at all, but it is the big theme in my life right now. And like anything, once you're looking for something, you find it, or you find the lack of it, everywhere you look.

Part of why I'm seeing it everywhere now is because I'm just coming around to the realization that I don't really want to need grace. And all of a sudden, now I can see that I never have been very comfortable with the idea. I don't really trust that people will show me grace. I don't show it to myself well, and when I'm doing very poorly, I don't show it to anyone else well, either.

Right now everywhere I turn is another reminder of grace, or of the space where grace should be. I have a friend who wants me to pray for a situation in her life over and over. Same situation. She calls me, emails me: please pray! I get annoyed with these messages, and while I was talking to Aaron about it, I heard myself say, "I don't *have* to pray for her. And I'm tired of her demanding that I do. She made a boatload of terrible decisions, and now I *have* to pray about it?"

Uh-oh. So in my economy, we earn the right to be prayed for by making all the right decisions? Practically speaking, if we all made all the right decisions, we wouldn't generally need prayer, would we? But more than that, who am I? Is it my job to decide who does and who doesn't deserve to be prayed for, based on the tokens they've put into the good-decision meter? My friend and I are bound together by our common love for Christ and common acceptance of his grace.

It gets even worse, actually. The thing is, she asked for my advice, many years ago, and went against it. This situation wouldn't exist had she taken my advice. So now my small, ugly self doesn't want to pray for her. Something about making one's bed and lying in it. I gave her what comes easily to me: advice. She didn't take it, and now she wants something that's harder for me to give: prayer.

That's a graceless way to live, where everything is an opportunity to achieve or fail. It's exhausting to live like that, where everything's a performance, and you can't trust the people in your life to give you a break or to give you a second chance or to give you what you really are longing for, which is grace.

I don't like the idea that someone can judge me and that I have to depend on their grace. I want to take that power out of their hands. I hate to think about the fact that the people who love me show me grace for all my faults. I prefer to believe instead that the math works: that there are good things about me and hard things about me, but that they've checked the math and because I'm funny enough, they can let go of how terrible I look most days, or that if I'm interesting enough, the fact that my house is dirty isn't such a big deal. But that kind of math is specifically antigrace. Grace isn't about netting out on the right side of things.

If arithmetic is numbers, and if algebra is numbers and letters, then grace is numbers, letters, sounds, and tears, feelings and dreams. Grace is smashing the calculator, and using all the broken buttons and pieces to make a mosaic.

Grace isn't about having a second chance; grace is having so many chances that you could use them through all eternity and never come up empty. It's when you finally realize that the other shoe isn't going to drop, ever. It's the moment you feel as precious and handmade as every star, when you feel, finally, at home for the very first time.

Grace is when you finally stop keeping score and when you realize that God never was, that his game is a different one entirely. Grace is when the silence is so complete that you can hear your own heartbeat, and right within your ribs, God's beating heart, too.

I used to think that the ability to turn back time would be the greatest possible gift, so that I could undo all the things I wish I hadn't done. But grace is an even better gift, because it allows me to do more than just erase; it allows me to become more than I was when I did those things. It's forgiveness without forgetting, which is much sweeter than amnesia.

So these days, I'm on the lookout for grace, and I'm especially on the lookout for ways that I withhold grace from myself and from other people. At first, showing people grace makes you feel powerful, like scattering candy from a float in a parade—grace for you, grace for you. You become almost giddy, thinking of people in generous ways, allowing for their faults, absorbing minor irritations. You feel great, and then you start to feel just ever so slightly superior, because you're so incredibly evolved and gracious.

But then inevitably something happens, and it usually involves you confronting one of your worst selves, often in public, and you realize that you're not throwing candy off a float to a nameless, dirty public, but rather that you are that nameless, dirty public, and that you are starving and on your knees, praying for a little piece of sweetness, just one mouthful of grace.

thirteen

TWENTY-FIVE

Here are a few thoughts on being twenty-five-ish, some that I knew, because smart older people gave me good advice, and some that I really wish I had known, that those smart older people probably did tell me, and that I lost track of along the way.

I know that age is, of course, one of the most arbitrary ways of measuring a person. I have friends in their sixties who continually teach me about discovery and possibility, and friends in their young twenties who are as crotchety and set in their ways as Archie Bunker. Age, like numbers on a scale and letters on a report card, tells us very little of who we are. You decide every year exactly how young and how old you want to be.

When you're twenty-five-ish, you're old enough to know what kind of music you love, regardless of what your last boyfriend or roommate always used to play. You know how to walk in heels, how to tie a necktie, how to give a good toast at a wedding, and how to make something for dinner. You don't have to think much about skin care, home ownership, or your retirement plan.

Your life can look a lot of different ways when you're twenty-five: single, dating, engaged, married. You are working in dream jobs, pay-the-bills jobs, and downright horrible jobs. You are young enough to believe that anything is possible, and you are old enough to make that belief a reality.

Now is the time to figure out what kind of work you love to do. What are you good at? What makes you feel alive? What do you dream about? You can go back to school now, switch directions entirely. You can work for almost nothing, or live in another country, or volunteer long hours for something that moves you. There will be a time when finances and schedules make this a little trickier, so do it now. Try it, apply for it, get up and do it.

When I was twenty-five, I was in my third job in as many years—all in the same area at a church, but the responsibilities were different each time. I was frustrated at the end of the third year, because I didn't know exactly what I wanted to do next. I didn't feel like I'd found my place yet. I met with my boss, who was in his fifties. I told him how anxious I was about finding the one perfect job for me, and quick. He asked me how old I was, and when I told him I was twenty-five, he told me that I couldn't complain to him about finding the right job until I was thirty-two. In his opinion, it takes about ten years after college to find the right fit, and anyone who finds it earlier than that is just plain lucky.

So use every bit of your ten years: try things, take classes, start over. One of my oldest friends, Jenny, got a degree in child psychology from Harvard, and has worked for years at a bunch of fancy companies as a client account manager. A few years ago, she finally realized that what she's always loved is helping to heal people through massage. Now after work and on weekends, she's the world's best-educated massage therapist, building up her clientele with every passing month, and happier than she's ever been.

My dear friend Rachel has been a makeup artist since she was eighteen, and after ten years, she decided that what she really wants to be is a therapist. So she's doing it now, getting her bachelor's degree, making plans for her master's, doing makeup all the while to pay for school. That's what this time is for, to figure those things out.

Now is also the time to get serious about relationships. And "serious" might mean walking away from the ones that don't give you everything you need. Some of the most life-shaping decisions you make in this season will be about walking away from *good-enough*, in search of *can't-live-without*. One of the only truly devastating mistakes you can make in this season is staying with the wrong person even though you know he or she is the wrong person. It's not fair to that person, and it's not fair to you.

My friend Chrissie and her boyfriend were together for ten years, since college. He's a great guy, but throughout their relationship, several people had told Chrissie that they observed a fundamental mismatch. They didn't fit together like puzzle pieces. They didn't fit together at all. But she stayed, out of love and hope and commitment, and then he proposed. And they just couldn't get the wedding planned.

They couldn't agree on where or when or how many people, so they stopped planning for a while. In the meantime, she went to South Africa with a group from our church to work with AIDS orphans, and while she was there, she felt alive and full of purpose for the first time in years. When she returned, her fiancé wasn't all that interested in hearing about it.

All the things her friends had been saying for years clicked into place, and a few weeks later, she gave back the ring. She's literally like a new person these days, full of bright energy, hope, clarity. And those things are worth a whole lot more than a diamond from the wrong man, even if he's a really good man, like this one was.

Twenty-five is also a great time to start counseling, if you haven't already, and it might be a good round two of counseling if it's been awhile. You might have just enough space from your parents to start digging around your childhood a little bit. Unravel the knots that keep you from living a healthy whole life, and do it now, before any more time passes.

Twenty-five is the perfect time to get involved in a church that you love, no matter how different it is from the one you were a part of growing up. Be patient and prayerful, and decide that you're going to be a person who grows, who seeks your own faith, who lives with intention. Set your alarm on Sunday mornings, no matter how late you were out on Saturday night. It will be dreadful at first, and then after a few weeks, you'll find that you like it, that the pattern of it fills up something inside you.

Try different kinds of communities, different sizes and denominations and traditions. My friend Monica grew up in a community church in Northern California, and now she's an elder at a Lutheran church in Reno because she appreciates the history and structure of this new context. Our friends Kelly and Amy grew up in nondenominational churches, and now have spent a number of years as passionate volunteers at the Presbyterian church in their neighborhood.

I know that most people need a season of space, a time to take a step back and evaluate the spiritual context of their youth. I didn't go to church for a long season in college, and that space and freedom was so important for me. It gave me the perspective I needed to find my own faith. But it's very easy for a season of space to turn into several years without any kind of spiritual groundedness. It's easy to wake up several years from now and find yourself unable to locate that precious, faith-filled part of your heart and history, because it slowly disintegrated over months and years. Don't do that. Do whatever you have to do to connect with God in a way that feels authentic and truthful to you. Do it now, so that you don't regret the person you become, little by little, over time, without it.

This is the thing: when you start to hit twenty-eight or thirty, everything starts to divide, and you can see very clearly two kinds of people: on one side, people who have used their twenties to learn and grow, to find God and themselves and their deep dreams, people who know what works and what doesn't, who have pushed through to become real live adults.

And then there's the other kind, who are hanging on to college, or high school even, with all their might. They've stayed in jobs they hate because they're too scared to get another one. They've stayed with men or women who are good but not great because they don't want to be lonely. They mean to find a church, they mean to develop honest, intimate friendships, they mean to stop drinking like life is one big frat party. But they don't do those things, so they live in kind of an extended adolescence, no closer to adulthood than they were when they graduated college.

Don't be like that. Don't get stuck. Move, travel, take a class, take a risk. Walk away, try something new. There is a season for wildness and a season for settledness, and this is neither. This season is about becoming. Don't lose yourself at happy hour, but don't lose yourself on the corporate ladder either.

Stop every once in a while and go out to coffee or climb in bed with your journal. Ask yourself some good questions like, Am I proud of the life I'm living? What have I tried this month? What have I learned about God this year? What parts of my childhood faith am I leaving behind, and what parts am I choosing to keep with me for this leg of the journey? Do the people I'm spending time with give me life, or make me feel small? Is there any brokenness in my life that's keeping me from moving forward?

These years will pass much more quickly than you think they will. You will go to lots of weddings, and my advice, of course, is to dance your pants off at every single one. I hope you go to very few funerals. You'll watch TV and run on the treadmill and go on dates, some of them great and some of them terrible. Time will pass, and all of a sudden, things will begin to feel a little more serious. You won't be old, of course. But you will want to have some things figured out, and the most important things only get figured out if you dive into them now.

For a while in my early twenties, I felt like I woke up a different person every day, and was constantly confused about which one, if any, was the real me. I feel more and more like myself with each passing year, for better and for worse, and you'll find that, too. Every year, you will trade a little of your perfect skin and your ability to look great without exercising for wisdom and peace and groundedness, and every year the trade will be worth it. I promise.

Now is your time. Become, believe, try. Walk closely with people you love, and with other people who believe that God is very good and life is a grand adventure. Don't spend time with people who make you feel like less than you are. Don't get stuck in the past, and don't try to fast-forward yourself into a future you haven't yet earned. Give today all the love and intensity and courage you can, and keep traveling honestly along life's path.

fourteen

THIN PLACES

It's Advent right now, and this year especially, I'm really thankful for Advent. Advent is about waiting, anticipating, yearning. Advent is the question, the pleading, and Christmas is the answer to that question, the response to the howl. There are moments in this season when I don't feel a lot like Christmas, but I do feel like Advent.

Advent gives us another option beyond false Christmas cheer or Scrooge. Advent says the baby is coming, but he isn't here yet, that hope is on its way, but the yearning is still very real. Sometimes, depending on what we've lost this year, Advent is what saves us from giving up on Christmas and all its buoyant twinkling-light hope forever. Advent allows us to tell the truth about what we're grieving, without giving up on the gorgeous and extravagant promise of Christmas, the baby on his way.

My mother is Irish, and when I was in college, I studied Irish literature and poetry in Ireland for a little while. So based on both my own Irish heritage and my own extensive research, I can say with some authority that the Irish have given us many wonderful gifts—among them, of course, whiskey and U2. Also among them, the Celtic mystical tradition. One of my favorite Celtic ideas is the concept of thin places. A thin place, according to the Celtic mystics, is a place where the boundary between the natural world and the supernatural one is more permeable—thinner, if you will.

Sometimes they're physical places. There are places all over Ireland where people have said, if you stand here, if you face this direction, if you hike to the top of that ridge at just the right time of day, that's a thin place, a place where the passage between heaven and earth is a short one, a place where God's presence is almost palpable.

An alternate and possibly lesser known usage of the term "thin place" refers to those very rare dressing rooms, where somehow the light and the mirrors and the cosmos are all working together, and magically, miraculously, every pair of jeans I try on fits. I'll be honest, I've only encountered this kind of thin place a handful of times, but just like the mystical kind, once you've experienced it you keep going back over and over again, hoping for the same kind of magic.

I encountered a thin place in the Savvy section at the Nordstrom in Woodfield Mall, and I go back to it over and over, hoping. Most of the time it's just like any other dressing room, and I try not to cry when I'm forced to confront my underbutt under the bluish fluorescent light in the three-way mirror. But every so often, that dressing room is a thin place, and my belief and fervor in it are renewed, and I buy exorbitantly expensive jeans because of it. By the way, if you don't know what an *underbutt* is, then you don't have one. In that case, Merry Christmas to you.

But I digress. Thin places: places where the boundary between the divine world and the human world becomes almost nonexistent, and the two, divine and human, can for a moment, dance together uninterrupted. Some are physical places, and some aren't places at all, but states of being or circumstances or seasons.

Christmas is a thin place, a season during which even the hardest-hearted of people think about what matters, when even the most locked-up individuals loosen their grasps for just a moment, in the face of the deep beauty and hope of Christmas. The shimmer of God's presence, not always plainly visible in our world, is more visible at Christmas.

When we find a thin place, anytime, anywhere, we should live differently in the face of it, because if we don't, we miss some of the best moments that life with God has to offer us. These thin places are gifts, treasures, and they're worth changing our lives for. Reach through from human to sacred every time the goodness of this season moves you. A thin place is an opportunity to be more aware of the divine fingerprints all over this world, and Christmas is one invitation after another to do that.

When you hear music that pierces your spirit, thank God for the gift of music. When you witness generosity that reminds you of the deep goodness of humanity, thank God for the way he created us. When you feel a profound sense of beauty, thank God for it. When the traditions and smells and sounds of Christmas that you love and wait for all year long overwhelm you and you think, *I love this world we live in*, thank

God for those things. When the faces of your children or your parents shock you with the love you feel for them, thank God.

There's another kind of thin place, and we find ourselves in these places when our lives and our hearts are broken open. Brokenness has a way of allowing the supernatural into our lives in the same way that deep joy or great beauty do—and maybe, I'm finding, even more.

Let me be clear: brokenness doesn't automatically bring us to the thin place, the sacred place where God's breath and touch are closer than our own skin. Heartbreak brings us lots of places—to despair, to bitterness, to emptiness, to numbness, to isolation. But because God is just that good, if we allow the people who love us to walk with us right through the broken-ness, it can also lead to a deep sense of God's presence. When things fall apart, the broken places allow all sorts of things to enter, and one of them is the presence of God.

For some people, this Christmas is, if I can stretch the phrase, doubly thin. It's Christmas—one kind of thin place, and it's a season of loss, an entirely different kind of thin place. Maybe it's the first Christmas without a family member or dear friend, and your heart has been so wholly battered that it allows God's presence and voice to seep into it at every turn. Or maybe a relationship broken this year hangs over the season like a veil. You are alone, freshly. A close friend of mine will celebrate her first Christmas alone, because her divorce became final earlier this year, and the man she fell in love with, hard, just after that, walked out of her life as quickly as he walked into it. She says that the loneliness is deafening sometimes.

I don't know what you've lost this year: a life, a friend, a child, a dream, a job, a home. I don't know what's broken your heart this year, but I do know that whatever it is, you may feel the loss of it even more acutely at Christmas.

I believe deeply that God does his best work in our lives during times of great heartbreak and loss, and I believe that much of that rich work is done by the hands of people who love us, who dive into the wreckage with us and show us who God is, over and over and over.

There are years when the Christmas spirit is hard to come by, and it's in those seasons when I'm so thankful for Advent. Consider it a less flashy but still very beautiful way of being present to this season. Give up for a while your false and failing attempts at merriment, and thank God for thin places, and for Advent, for a season that understands longing and loneliness and long nights. Let yourself fall open to Advent, to anticipation, to the belief that what is empty will be filled, what is broken will be repaired, and what is lost can always be found, no matter how many times it's been lost.

fifteen

GIFTS, UNDER THE TREE AND OTHERWISE

Some of the best Christmas gifts we give and receive are the ones that have nothing to do with wrapping paper and twinkling lights. To be clear, I am totally a gift person. I know that every year, and this one more than ever, there are those people who think we shouldn't buy gifts at all, or that we should only give handmade gifts, or coupons for backrubs or something. I like that idea, and certainly there's something to be said for curtailing any wild overspending in the name of the Baby Jesus, but all the same, I love to buy gifts. And I'm not down on receiving them either.

I did buy the cutest scarves for a few of my best girlfriends. I met a woman in Nashville recently, and by that I mean I saw her in the Starbucks at my hotel, and I followed her all the way down the hall to talk to her about her scarf. She was really nice even though I completely stalked her, and she pointed me to a store a few blocks away where I bought several darling scarves. I am generally against the matching gift—you know, lotion for everyone. But one of the funny things about our life this Christmas is that each of the four couples in our housechurch will be living in different parts of the country by January, and I kind of like the idea of each of these women, in different places all over the country, rocking their matching scarves.

I don't come from a church with many traditions, but there are a few, and our Christmas tradition is my favorite one. The services are different every year, and to be perfectly honest, some have worked better than others. One year, it was kind of an urban, "street" Christmas, kind of edgy and dark. We learned the hard way that that's not really the vibe people are looking for at Christmas. Another year, an attempt at realism left the men in our community deeply troubled during the birth part of the story. One man I know said that he learned more about how babies get born at church that year than he did in the actual delivery room with his wife.

Whatever the service, though, it always ends the same way. The very last song is always "Silent Night," and my dad, who's the pastor at our church, always tells people that this is their chance to express love, through words and hugs, to the people that they came with. For lots of people, it's the only time all year that they actually look one another in the eye and say, *I love you*, or *I'm thankful for you*, or *You matter to me*. I love those moments. I love looking out over the room and seeing people hug and hearing the buzz of all those words, and in the last few years, I've tried to incorporate that spirit into all of my relationships, beyond the moment in the service.

I'm hit-or-miss at best on Christmas cards, having totally abandoned the idea the last few years. I know that you all probably sent them out the day after Thanksgiving, and that they have little handmade ornaments inside or something, but some years the idea of all the addresses and the photo and the stamps just put me absolutely over the edge. On those years, though, I do still buy one little box of cards to give to the people I love, and it guarantees that I sit down, right in the midst of the insanity of the season, and tell my family and my closest friends how deeply their love has affected me. I'll sit down and think about our babysitter, and how profound my gratitude toward her is for the way she cares for our son. This is, I believe, one of the best ways we can honor the season.

Don't let this season pass without taking the time and energy and creativity and risk to speak plainly with the people you love about exactly what they bring to your life. You may come from one of those families that consider a wink and a handshake true intimacy, but if Christmas hinges on traditions, please consider beginning a new family tradition. Use the sacredness and the deep beauty of this season as a shameless excuse to tell people you love how much you love them. You can get away with anything at Christmas—we wear earrings that light up and eat cookies for three meals a day; this is your time to be a little wacky and get away with it, certainly.

This season matters. Christmas is a time when God's presence is more palpable than any other time of the year. It's also a time when what we've lost is more present to us, when the pain or the loneliness or the fear are more present than any other time. It's a glorious, beautiful time and also one in which even the smallest kindnesses can transform us. It's worth more than pushing and rushing and perfecting your decorations or your homemade cookies.

If what it takes for you this year to be present in this sacred, thin place, to feel the breath and presence of a Holy God, is to forgo the cookies and the cards and the rushing and the lists, then we'll be all right with cookies from the store and a few less gifts. It would be a great loss for you to miss this season, the soul of it, because you're too busy pushing and rushing. And it would be a great loss if the people in your life receive your perfectly wrapped gifts, but not your love or your full attention or your spirit.

This is my prayer for us, that we would give and receive the most important gifts this season—the palpable presence of a Holy God, the kindness of well-chosen words, the generosity of spirit and soul.

My prayer is that what you've lost, and what I've lost this year, will fade a little bit in the beauty of this season, that for a few moments at least, what is right and good and worth believing will outshine all the darkness, within us and around us.

And I hope that someone who loves you gives you a really cute scarf.

Merry Christmas.

sixteen

COMING HOME

One month ago today, the movers were unloading our furniture and boxes. We were trying to figure out the locations of light switches and where the piano should go. We slept fitfully that first night, because of the funny noises and silences in an unfamiliar home, and because Henry was sleeping in his big-boy racecar bed for the first time—a new bed and a new room. And now, somehow, it's been a month.

In the long expanse between the planning and the actual moving, I dreamed about this house, and specifically, I dreamed about cooking in this house. I was so excited to stop traveling for a while, and to really live in a home, to be able to buy vegetables and not worry that they'd go bad while I was gone, Aaron eating frozen meals night and day in my absence. I wanted people around our table, after a season of eating most of my meals in airports and hotel rooms, or collapsing onto the couch with hummus and crackers to watch a movie with Henry at the end of a hurried day.

And yesterday I realized that my dream has more than come true. On our very first night, my mom brought over thick roasted vegetable soup, and we sat around our table with my parents and Aaron's parents, telling funny moving stories, filled with gratitude for this home, and for all the answered prayers that it represents.

Since then we've had polenta with rosemary tomato sauce with Matt and Casey and their kids, eggs and bacon and blueberry sausages when Joe and Emily visited, and a long, lazy breakfast with scones and roasted potatoes with Alan and Sara and their family when they visited. We've had edamame and pot stickers and chicken teriyaki, and Dijon-and-thyme marinated chicken with sweet potato and apple gratin. When Darren and Brandy and their darling girls came over, we had basil and parmesan risotto with buttered peas. We celebrated my mother-in-law's birthday with enchiladas and black bean salad. At one point, I went on a major soup kick, so in one week, we had roasted garlic and potato soup, rosemary tomato and rice soup, black bean and corn soup, and Aaron's favorite, curried sweet potato and apple soup.

Before we moved, I had been dreaming about three things: feeding people, quiet writing mornings, and lots of time with Henry. Check, check, check. Gratitude, gratitude, gratitude.

I know, really, that a month is nothing—a blip, a flash. But I also know that a few of the things that have been frantic and running around in me for the last few years are slowing down. And of course, a few aren't. I'm still the same old me, wriggling with self-doubt most days, and that's not something you leave at the state line, as much as I wish it was. But at the same time, some very important things have shifted.

Recently I saw a friend I hadn't seen in years. "I heard you're engaged!" I cried as I hugged her, exuberantly. "Congratulations!"

"I'm not engaged," she said. "I was, and I'm not anymore." Oh, heavens. I started to apologize, but she put her hand on my arm and interrupted me.

"It's all right," she said. "Breaking the engagement was the first conscious decision of my life." What an extraordinary statement. And as I spent time with her, I could see the truth of her words, the bloom of her eyes and skin and spirit. She had made a fundamental, defining choice, and it brought life and hope to her words and her world.

Her words rang in my ears because I wanted to make a conscious decision of my own, and her words gave a name to something I'd been aching for for a long time. Many of the key decisions in my life have been pretty natural—they sort of fell into being, or came about as I traveled life's path. Many of them just seemed like the next right thing, the most natural progression. But this move back to my hometown and the church I grew up in, as much as it looks natural to the outside observer, this move was one of the first conscious decisions of my life. This is what I wanted, what I prayed for, what I asked for from my husband.

For one of the first times in my life, as I thought and prayed about the possibility of this move, I became very quiet and still, and looked over my life like I was panning for gold in a river, seeing every single thing, the dirt and the water and the slubby green moss on the rocks. I looked and listened and wrote, and what I found is that I wanted to be *home*.

Not everyone, I'm learning, has a deep sense of home. But for me, even after four years in Santa Barbara and six years in Grand Rapids, Chicago is still my home.

I was wrestling with the idea of home, and by wrestling, I mean I asked everyone I knew or ran into, drove them crazy with questions about their own sense of home, their memories and associations with the topic. We had dinner with our friends Doug and Shelley, and after dinner, over a rich baked rice pudding I still think about, I asked them about home. They both grew up in Minneapolis, got married and had kids there, and then life and work took them to Dallas. But Doug realized that whenever he watched the weather, wherever he was, he was looking at Minnesota on the weather map. Whenever his plane arrived at the Minneapolis airport, even if he was just connecting to go on to another place, he felt like he was home.

That's how I feel about Chicago. Even after six years in Grand Rapids, when people asked me where I was from, I said Chicago, and then added that I currently lived in Grand Rapids, making it sound like I was cooling my heels there for six weeks or so, not that I owned a home and a lawnmower and had a tailor, a pediatrician, and a regular breakfast place there.

And it wasn't that I didn't like Grand Rapids. It's something under that, something a little more wiggly. It's that Chicago is familiar to me on a deep level, like when you recognize the melody of a song before you even realize there's music playing. Grand Rapids grew on me, in all sorts of ways. I settled in, had a baby there, found a few coffee shops and restaurants and friends that made me feel like we were building a little life there. But when the topic of home came up, home was Chicago.

And after the chaos and wildness of the last few years, I wanted to be home. I wanted a small house with lots of windows and no mice. I wanted to write, and to be with Henry, to travel less and cook more. I wanted to be a part of a church again, to volunteer and show up every week, to feel connected to the rhythm of it.

And today I'm filled with gratitude. For a woman who doesn't always know what she wants, I believed in a deep way this time around that this decision would lead us to our best future. I thought about it, wrote about it, prayed for it, talked to Aaron and to the people we walk closely with every step of the way. And here we are, one month into this beautiful new season, the one I held in my heart and my mind for so long. It isn't perfect, but I wasn't looking for perfect. This is what I've wanted, on a very deep level, and on an icy cold winter day, I'm overwhelmed by the sweetness of it. It feels good to be home.

seventeen

WHAT MIGHT HAVE BEEN

Today all I can think about is what might have been. It's a Saturday, bitter cold and bright, harsh, splintering. We're doing normal Saturday things, and since we recently moved into our new house, "normal" includes unpacking the remaining boxes, assembling furniture, making endless Target and Ikea lists.

Today is the day that would have been my due date, had my pregnancy been a healthy one. Nine months ago, the world was so different. I was so different. The concept of pregnancy was so different to me, so innocent. Of course I knew women who had miscarried: my mother, my cousin, my friends. But like anything, when it happens to you, it's like waking up to a conversation you've heard before and only now grasp, and you realize entirely anew what they were talking about, what they were trying to find the words to describe.

So that's today, the day of what might have been. Someday we might have another child. But we'll never have a child born on January 31, 2009. The baby I found out about on Memorial Day weekend, the happy secret I shared with Aaron on the phone, standing outside the Phoenix Street Café, the baby I carried inside me to Fiji to visit Todd and Joe on the boat—that baby will never be. And it seems worth stopping for today, just for a moment.

For me, as well, the specifics of the miscarriage changed me from one kind of mother to another. It's a broad sisterhood of women who don't have easy conceptions and pregnancies, but to be honest, I liked being in the other group. It was so deeply moving to me that my body nurtured and nourished Henry, delivering him safely into the world, whole and healthy, and this miscarriage and its aftermath have forced me to ask some questions: Did my body fail me? Did I somehow fail it? We've had such a tenuous relationship in the past, my body and I; was this a breach of trust?

I went to a wedding six months after the miscarriage. The wedding was absolutely perfect, the first of my ten small group girls to get married, a sweet celebration on a hot Austin night. Christel was gorgeous, all eyelashes and happy tears, and we all danced together and took pictures and laughed. And then for a little while, Kristin, another one of the girls from my small group, left, walked to the front of the old house alone, stood on the sidewalk, listening to the music in the distance, heart heavy with what might have been.

Kristin does this at every wedding. She dances and laughs and hugs and smiles for pictures, and then, at one point or another, she slips away and lets a few tears fall for the maid of honor who will never stand at her own wedding someday.

Kristin's sister Laurie ended her own life four years ago. They were stepsisters and best friends. And then when they were both twenty, Laurie chose to end her life in a heartbreaking, confusing tangle of hurt and accusation and broken friendships. I remember the first everything—the one-month mark, the first birthday after she was gone, the one-year mark.

Kristin, of course, remembers Laurie all the time, but the ache is never more acute than at weddings, because when Kristin gets married, the sister she dreamed about weddings with for years won't stand with her on that day. Weddings, more than anything else, bring her to what might have been.

And now Kristin and her fiancé, Sean, are getting married, and she's thinking about how to walk through the months of her engagement and the day of her wedding without her sister. The ache for her sister has deepened in the season before the wedding. Kristin decided she won't have a maid of honor, so that no one will stand in the place of Laurie's memory on the day that the two sisters had dreamed about for so long.

The night Sean proposed, Kristin started to cry in between phone calls to friends and family. Sean asked her to dance in the living room, surrounded by the flowers and candles he'd set up for the proposal, and as they danced, she realized the one phone call she still wanted to make was to her sister Laurie. Kristin felt both angry and sad in that moment, remembering Laurie's exuberant phone call to her just a few months before her death—"I'm engaged!" Kristin wanted so badly to make that same call to her sister and best friend that night, and it felt deeply unfair that Laurie wasn't there to pick up the phone.

If you've been marked by what might have been, you don't forget. You know the day, the years. You know when the baby would have been born. You know exactly what anniversary you'd be celebrating, if the wedding had happened. You know exactly how old she'd be right now, if she were still alive. You'll never forget the last time you saw your child, or the last time *cancer* was a word about someone else's life, or the day that changed absolutely everything. It makes the calendar feel like a minefield, like you're constantly tiptoeing over explosions of grief until one day you hit one, shattered by what might have been.

On most days, for me, it's all right. We'll have another baby someday. I hope we do. But for today, for a minute, it's not all right. I understand that God is sovereign, that bodies are fragile and fallible. I understand that grief mellows over time, and that guarantees aren't part of human life, as much as we'd like them to be. But on this day, looking out at the harsh white sky of a Chicago winter, I'm crying just a little for what might have been.

I'll get up from here, wash my face and hands, peer in at Henry while he sleeps, a sweaty, unruly little boy, dreams of dragons and Buzz Lightyear flickering behind his eyelids. I'll have dinner in the city with my oldest friends tonight, toasting the first time in years we've lived in the same town. Life will keep moving, exactly as it should. No one might ever notice January 31, and what it means for me. But I'll always know.

I don't know what date it is for you—what broke apart on that day, what was lost, what memories are pinned forever to that day on that calendar. But I hope that, like Kristin, on that day you leave the dance floor and hold yourself open and tender to the memories for just a moment. As one who grieves today, I grieve with you, for whatever you've lost, too, for what might have been.

eighteen

HAPPY MOTHER'S DAY

There are a thousand things I learned from my mother. I learned to set an elegant table. I learned that your world will never be small if you love to read, because you can be anyone, anywhere, at any period in history, if you love to read. I learned the importance of prayer, the importance of fresh flowers, and how to appreciate poetry. My mom taught me that age is something to celebrate and not something to fear, and when Henry was born, she taught me how to rock a newborn to sleep.

What I know now is that almost every woman mothers, in one way or another. I guess I used to think it was an all-at-once thing, that you go to the hospital a woman and come out a mother, like going through a car wash with a dirty car and coming out with a clean one.

But now that I am a mother, what is very clear to me is that I have been mothered by a whole tribe of women, some who had children of their own, and some who didn't. I thank God for each one of them, and thank them for mothering me when I needed it, and for giving me such a rich variety of images for what it means to be a mother.

And also now that I am a mother, I understand what Mother's Day is about: it's about looking through our lives and recognizing the act of mothering everywhere we see it, and more than that, recognizing that when any of us mother—when we listen, nurture, nourish, protect—we're doing sacred work.

One of the most important things I've learned about mothering goes back to something I heard several years ago from my friend Nancy, who gave me her time and her wisdom just after I graduated from college. She told me that when you compare yourself to another person, you always lose, and at the same time the other person always loses, too. Each of us has been created by the hands of a holy God, and our stories and the twists and turns of our lives, the things that are hard for us, and the things that come naturally, are as unique to us as our own fingerprints. She told me that one way to ensure a miserable life is to constantly measure your own life by the lives of the people around you.

I was in my early twenties when she first talked with me about comparison. When you're a woman in your early twenties, you compare grades if you're in college or grad school. You compare sizes and weight, and whose degree is more impressive. You compare boyfriends—their cars and jobs and social skills. You compare apartments, menus at your dinner parties, and at a certain point, engagement rings.

And then you have children, and you, regrettably, begin to compare children. It starts, actually, with pregnancy. Everyone wants to talk about how much weight you gained, in comparison to how much weight they gained. In what other possible scenario is this an appropriate topic of conversation?

I think that the people who ask are really just looking for an opportunity to brag about how little weight they gained. I don't ask. I have a very strict *Don't Ask, Don't Tell* policy. My husband doesn't even know how much weight I gained when I was pregnant. I've never been so thankful for doctor-patient confidentiality laws. You just tell every pregnant woman you see that she's glowing, even if she's the size of a Volkswagen, and leave it at that.

Another thing that's very important, apparently, when you have a child, is to keep track of exactly how many words they can say. I have one friend who asks all the time, "How many words does he have?" And I think to myself, um, a lot? Way more than I need on some days? And do you count each different word, or, for example, if he says the same word, over and over, nine hundred times in a row, is that nine hundred words?

My friend Ginger came over the other day, and I was making lunch for Henry and her daughter, Samantha. I gave them each their Dino Bites and their organic fruit leather, and I was trying to find something vegetable for them. I was looking in the freezer, and in the pantry. And Ginger was coaching me, "Maybe some peas? Or little baby carrots?" And finally Ginger said, "You know what? Even if you put them on her plate, she won't eat them. I don't actually give her a vegetable every single day at lunch." And I said, "Me neither! Me neither! I do it at dinner, I swear, but I don't always give him a vegetable at lunch." You would have thought in that moment that we were confessing our deepest, darkest secrets to one another.

I've known Ginger since I was thirteen. We were in each other's weddings. She knows all the things I did in high school that my parents still don't know about. Why were we faking each other out about vegetables for two-year-olds? Because we both believed, in that moment, that moms should be perfect. That we should be perfect. That every meal must have a vegetable, that vegetable must be organic, that our homes should look like the Pottery Barn Kids catalog, and that somehow everyone else is able to pull it off, even if we can't.

We slip into believing that it's better to strive for perfection than to accept and offer one another grace. Back once again to grace, the spiritual theme of my year. What I need as a mother is grace. God's grace, that allows me to fail and try again, that allows me to ask for help when I don't have the wisdom or patience I need, that reminds me we're not alone in this, and that God loves my son even more than I do. And grace from other mothers. I need grace and truth-telling and camaraderie from other moms. I need us to tell the truth about how hard it is, and I need us to help each other, instead of hiding behind the pretense and pressure of perfection.

There are some moments these days, since the miscarriage, when I feel like a failure because my body wasn't able to do what so many other women's bodies can. I see them with their kids, a year apart, one after another. That will never be true for me and for our family. I'll always remember, even if we do have more children someday, the loss we experienced last summer. But what has healed me more than anything else are the stories of other women who have experienced similar things. I've needed grace, and I've needed women who share their sorrows with me, and allow me to share my own.

My friend Nancy lives in California now, and when she heard that I lost the baby, she sent me a card. It said, "Rest, heal, you will be a mother again." And when I read it, I put my head down and sobbed, in sadness, but also in gratitude, for a woman who knows me well enough, even after all these years, to know what words will stitch me back together when my heart is broken.

So while I'm making a laundry list of all the things I need—grace, truth-telling, confessions about vegetables— here's another one: I need older, more experienced moms to help me. Seriously, I was not trained for this. Some women have child psychology degrees, or nursing backgrounds, or elementary education degrees. I think this would be very helpful. I have an English and French degree. My kid speaks a pretty limited amount of English and absolutely no French.

I am so deeply happy to be back in the same town as my mother and my mother-in-law, but for the first two years of Henry's life, I literally loitered in the baby section at Target, trying to make eye contact with strangers. I'd start with something obvious, like "Oh, do you use those bottles? Are those good bottles?" And if they answered with even remote friendliness, I'd push my luck: "What do you think about sleep schedules, just while I have you here? And you know, what do you think about public versus private education and which brand of car seat do you prefer and will I ever feel normal again?"

So if you're a mom, and your kids are grown, and you've been through this drill before, those of us who are still in the day to day of very hands-on parenting really need your help. If you see someone like me in the baby aisle at Target or at church or in your neighborhood, we really are every bit as desperate as we look, and we could use some help. And a nap. And a shower. But mostly, just a little help.

Let's think about grace—grace from a God who loves us and values us and picks us up every time we fall, with just exactly the same love and tenderness you feel when you pick up your kids after they've fallen. And the grace we show one another when we finally drop the comparisons and the catalog images and really walk with one another, on the good days and the bad days. Let's think about honesty and helping and telling our stories. Let's give each other a break and a little help and some soft places to land.

If you're a mom, what you do is nurture and protect and give grace. You do it all the time, and it's very important, because it reminds us, in daily, tangible ways how God nurtures and protects and gives grace. And maybe today the one who really needs that nurturing and protection and grace is you.

nineteen

SAY SOMETHING

When something bad happens, people say the wrong things so often. They say weird, hurtful things when they're trying to be nice. They say things that don't hurt until later, and then when they do begin to hurt, you can't get the words out of your mind. It's like a horror movie: everywhere you turn, those awful words are scrawled on every wall.

But there's something worse than the things people say. It's much worse, I think, when people say nothing. When I lost my job, embarrassed and hurt and tender, I remember exactly who walked the other direction when they saw me at church and who walked toward me.

The same was true with my miscarriage. I can tell you to this day what people said and, much more hurtfully, who said nothing at all. Some people said really helpful, really loving things. Aaron's aunt sent me a letter that was so thoughtful and so healing. Dear friends from Texas and New York sent flowers. My friend Courtney told me that when she heard the news she cried, and the image of my old friend crying on my behalf touches me every time I think about it. Women I didn't know well at all sent me tender messages telling me about their experiences. My friends Katie and Kevin gave me a book that put words to my feelings and helped me move forward.

Some people didn't know what to say, and they said just that: "I heard what happened, and I don't know what to say." That is, I'm finding, a very good response. Because there was another group of people who said nothing. I love them, and I know they love me, and the point is not what they did or didn't do, exactly. The point is that they taught me something, and it's this: say something. Always say something. Now when a friend loses a job or when a heart is broken or when the test results are bad, even when I don't know what to say, I say something.

I don't know why a few people chose not to say anything in those seasons. But I do know that I've done the exact same thing too many times. I can remember some of them, and now I regret those moments very much. I remember someone mentioning an illness, a hospital stay, a treatment. I didn't really know what they were talking about, so I didn't ask questions. I remember hearing of a friend who lost a grandparent, and I prayed for them but couldn't find their address, so I didn't send a card. I remember getting a text about a friend's miscarriage, and feeling like a text back wasn't the best response. I told myself I'd call, but I didn't call for several days. I'm ashamed of those things, and now, however awkward, however stilted, I try to say something, every time.

I know we're busy. I know we forget sometimes. More than anything, I think, we so desperately don't want to say the wrong thing. It's impolite, we've been told, to bring up nasty topics like loss and sadness. But if we don't bring it up, what are we left with? We talk about the easy things, the happy things, the weather, and then we leave one another totally alone with the diagnosis or the divorce papers.

When you're mourning, when something terrible has happened, it's on your mind and right at the top of your heart all the time. It's genuinely shocking to you that the sun is still shining and that people are still chattering away on *Good Morning America*. Your world has changed, utterly, and it feels so incomprehensible that the bus still comes and the people in the cars next to you on the highway just drive along as if nothing's happened. When you're in that place, it's a gift to be asked how you're doing, and most of the time the answer comes tumbling out, like water over a broken dam, because someone finally asked, finally offered to carry what feels like an unbearable load with you.

Our friends Darren and Brandy came over this summer, and after dinner, after the kids were in bed, they asked about the church we left and the jobs we left. We hadn't known them for very long and hadn't talked about all that with anyone for ages. I started with the very short version, not wanting to bore them, wanting to move on quickly to a lighter topic. And then Brandy said, "We actually want to hear the whole story. We want to know you and understand who you are because of that season." We stayed up so late that night, and as I went to bed I realized what a gift it was to be asked. I'd never bring that season up, because it's a mess, totally not something you bring up with new friends. But it's part of our history, and it meant something to me that they wanted to understand it.

Say something, every time, and ask the simplest questions: How are you? What was it like? What can I do? In my experience, you can never go wrong with flowers and food, even when someone insists that there's nothing at all you can do. I'd never come out and ask you to bring me a meal, but in a difficult season recently, we ate my mother-in-law's potato thyme soup and Jessie's coconut milk ice cream and September's chicken casserole for days on end, and we were thankful every time we opened the fridge and didn't have to think, our hearts and minds so full and troubled.

Flowers, I think, are always a good idea: new life in a vase. During a season of great loss for us, friends sent a gardenia in a beautiful glazed celery-colored pot. My track record with keeping plants alive is awful, but I tried my best, and then one morning, maybe two weeks later, I came around the corner and there it was: one perfect bloom. I almost cried, with relief that I hadn't killed it yet, and also with gratitude. From thousands of miles away, these friends and their kindness reminded me that new life always follows death.

A man I've known all my life recently lost his job—his job at the church where my husband leads worship and where my dad is a pastor. I was at the drugstore buying printer cartridges and suntan lotion, without makeup and in my pajamas. He didn't see me. I thought about leaving him alone, letting him shop in peace and not have to face me unexpectedly, one more person from church, one more person to explain it to.

But instead I walked down his aisle and said hello. After we talked about both our families, I told him that I'd heard about his job, and that I was so sorry. I asked how he was doing. I told him that I'd been through a kind of similar thing with my job a few years ago, and that I might understand some of the feelings he was feeling. He said it was good to hear from someone who'd been through a similar thing and was still standing. We talked for a while about what's next for him.

I know that I certainly didn't say anything profound. But I said something. I said something, as a way of being thankful to the people who said something to me when I needed it. I said something because I remember how much it mattered to me.

I don't believe that God's up in heaven making things go terribly wrong in our lives so that we learn better manners and better coping skills. But I do believe in something like composting for the soul: that if you can find life out of death, if you can use the smashed up garbage to bring about something new and good, however tiny, that's one of the most beautiful things there is.

I learned to say something. And I offer my apologies for all the times I didn't say something. I'm really sorry about that. For a whole bunch of not very good reasons, I didn't know better then. But I know better now.

So when there's bad news or scary news or when something falls apart, say something. Send a note. Send a text. Send flowers. And if you don't know what to say, try this: "I heard what happened, and I don't know what to say."

twenty

ON CRYING IN THE BATHROOM

I

There are two kinds of women: women who have cried in the bathroom, and women who haven't. What I mean by that first group is this: women who swear to their friends and husbands that they're not getting their hopes up this month, but they have actually absolutely checked the Due Date Calculator on babycenter.com eleven times just this week. I know, because these days I am a woman who cries in the bathroom.

Of course, all of us who cry in the bathroom *know* that there are all different kinds of crying. I know some women who cry when the test is positive. I know women who cry because it's the wrong time or the wrong man or because they fear they'll break their parents' hearts. I try to understand it,

126

but, you know, right now I don't, really, because sometimes pain makes us selfish, myopic, and utterly unable to understand people whose pain is different than ours. It shouldn't be that way. It should be that all pain softens us to all pain, but because we're so cracked-up, and because life is just that wicked sometimes, when all you want in the world is a positive pregnancy test, you can't see straight.

You regard your friend who is weeping over a surprise pregnancy a little bit like this: "Oh really? Oh, boo-hoo for you. How terrible that your body is so strong and healthy and working so incredibly well that it makes you babies when you don't even want them. I'm spending hours online reading long conspiracy theories about everything from antibiotics in milk to too much time in the hot tub, and in the meantime, your lush, perfect, fertile body just went ahead and started growing a baby without your even asking it to. Take your bursting belly of love and your fabulous pregnant cleavage away from me, because I feel as withered and dried up and hollowed out as a dead tree stump, and all your glittering pregnantness makes me want to cry in the bathroom all over again." Or, you know, something like that.

We do get that not everyone is thrilled to be pregnant, and we do at some point actually finally locate our empathy about what a surprise pregnancy means. But surprise pregnancies seem so specifically unfair, somehow, like their bodies are betraying them in just the perfectly opposite way our bodies are betraying us.

I do think it's doubly cruel that some of these major life events tend to happen all in the same seasons. There's the college application season, when we're all getting accepted or rejected right at the same time. I remember my shame and embarrassment about not being accepted to my dream school, and I remember that shame and embarrassment being so much more tender because one of my best friends had been accepted to that same school. We had been walking together, and I hit a dead end while she kept walking.

There's also the wedding season, when, for a couple of years, most of your Saturday nights involve Jordan almonds, chicken with wild rice, and dancing to "Brick House." I don't believe I've ever heard that song outside a wedding reception. Once I did hear it dedicated to the mother of the bride at a wedding reception in Mississippi, and my memory of that moment still makes me laugh out loud every time I think about it, even ten years later. Weddings are especially hard to go to if you've recently broken up with someone, or if it's been a long time since you've kissed someone and really meant it. Love and cherish, *blah blah blah*, when does cocktail hour start?

And then the next wave, a few years later, is the baby wave, a highly fraught, incredibly delicate process, both the biological part and the part where you announce your pregnancy, knowing that it will make someone else cry, possibly in front of you, but more likely in the car later, or after they hang up the phone. I've told and been told, been thoroughly happy, and have also been the one to cry in the car. For a while several of us commiserated every month, calling one another after we wiped our tears, but now that little band is smaller each month—Jessie is pregnant, now Larissa is pregnant, and while I'm thrilled for them, there are still a few of us who are left behind in that same circle, wondering who will leave next, for the land of bellies and baby gear.

We have already heard, by the way, that stress just makes it harder to get pregnant, and we've also heard the story about how as soon as you stopped trying, you got surprise pregnant. Thank you for mentioning that, though, over and over. Oh, just take down the stress level? Thank you, Mrs. I-read-online-too. Are you, in fact, a fertility specialist?

The first month, this time around, was the worst one. We had just moved and just started trying again, after the six months I had to wait after the miscarriage. I was absolutely sure I was pregnant. I was sick in the mornings, and I knew it was mostly from the prenatals, but I still relished it a little bit—morning sickness! Pregnant! And then I realized I wasn't pregnant, on the way to dinner with friends we barely knew, friends who had a two-year-old and a newborn, the darling family I wanted. I cried and cried in the car, and I used a baby wipe to fix my makeup in the driveway. I didn't know them well enough to tell them then.

That night I couldn't sleep, so I got out of bed and read a Ruth Reichl book I'd read before, just to be somewhere else, just to live in another world for a while. I put it down at a certain point and cried, alone in my silent living room.

I know it's incredibly common. I know that many women wait longer than I've waited. Two of my close friends miscarried last summer when I did, and both have miscarried again since then. I know that to have a strong, healthy boy like Henry means I have nothing to complain about, really. But what I feel is longing, plain old longing, like a country song, like loving someone who won't love you back, like a howl.

I I

The longing is reaching fever pitch right now because it's almost Memorial Day weekend, the weekend last year when I found out I was pregnant. I remember it all, every detail, and I'm hoping that history repeats itself, and also that it doesn't. Because I also remember the doctor's office and the storm and the tears and the awkward silences. I remember how badly I wanted to be alone, and how wrecked and closed down my body felt after the surgery.

So I'm hoping and remembering, and in the very same moment, talking myself down. *Don't think about it. Don't think about it.* It's all I can think about.

I know that most of us are longing for something. I know that longing is part of the deal, part of living in the not-yet-heaven. I know people who are longing to marry, who are longing to be healed from disease, longing for their children to come home, longing for the financial pressure to release. I get that longing is part of how we live.

But today I feel angry and boxed in, like the system is rigged against me and everywhere I turn, someone else's body is blooming with new life, while mine still, again, is not. I know it's not personal. But it all feels personal on some days. When you're afraid no one will ever love you, a friend who falls in love feels cruel. When your back is breaking under worry and fear about money, someone else's good fortune breaks your back just a little more.

That's why it's hard, I think, to rejoice with those who rejoice and mourn with those who mourn. I love that line from the Bible, but it's so incredibly difficult sometimes, because when you've got reason to rejoice, you forget what it's like to mourn, even if you swear you never will. And because when you're mourning, the fact that someone close to you is rejoicing seems like a personal affront.

I'll celebrate with my friends. I'll hold babies, buy baby gifts, ask them what it's like for them and really listen to the answer. I'll do it because it's the right thing to do, and because I can't ask them to mourn with me unless I'm willing to celebrate with them, as deeply painful as it is on some days. And my friends have done it for me, certainly; they stood in my wedding when they wanted to be brides, brought shower gifts when they wanted to be mothers. No one is exempt from the longing, and now, it seems, it's my turn.

III

Memorial Day weekend has come and gone, and this is what I'm realizing: one of the reasons I wanted to be pregnant now so badly is because I believed that doing it all over again exactly the same way, but with a different ending, a happy ending, would be such a beautiful story. So beautiful that I almost let myself start believing it was true. But it isn't true. I cried in the bathroom again on a windy Saturday afternoon, and then sat on the steps looking out at the water for a while, in disbelief and longing. It would have been such a beautiful story. I called Aaron and read some Joan Didion and watched the water.

And I realized something, as I tried to untangle my sadness and anger and confusion. I had believed that the miscarriage was an open wound that would only be healed by a healthy pregnancy. So I've been waiting on a pregnancy to move me out of this terrible season of loss. And I've been weighing down a pregnancy that doesn't even exist yet with truckloads of expectation and pressure. I realized that I need to close the wound now, and that it's unfair, to me and to an unknowable future, to leave it open any longer.

I decided, on that Saturday, looking out at the water, that the miscarriage is over, that that season has passed, and that a year was more than long enough. I decided that I wasn't waiting any longer for the next pregnancy to end that season for me.

My magical Memorial Day fantasy didn't have a happy ending. I didn't get to watch history repeat itself except better, with redemption, healing, and a newborn this time. But that's pretty much consistent with what we know about life, right? Not that really wanting something is wrong, but that a whole lot of life is spent picking up the pieces of any number of fantasies we've really wanted to believe. I'm still hoping for a happy ending, but if there is one for us, it will be a little off-kilter and not nearly as tidy and poetic as I'd hoped. It will carry inside it a whole lot of tears and longing, and a few good lessons learned watching the lake one Saturday afternoon.

I'll keep celebrating the good news with each friend and each new baby, until maybe I'm the only one left in that dwindling circle. And I'll ask for help and tenderness every time I find myself crying in the bathroom. And most important, I'll choose to believe that sometimes the happiest ending isn't the one you keep longing for, but something you absolutely cannot see from where you are.

twenty-one

HEADLINES AND LULLABIES

I usually try to view current events through the lens of general human progress, obscured sometimes by emotionally manipulative media trends. There are bad days and good ones, but we're generally on the right track, moving forward as a human family, as long as you take the long view.

That's what I usually say. But the news right now is such bad news. Sometimes I wonder if I should even watch it. I do, and I try to look for moments of integrity and bravery and triumph, believing that we are, on the whole, capable of great things, as individuals, as a nation, and as a human family. But it's becoming pretty difficult to maintain the assertion that it's all okay. That's a tough one to swallow if you watch the news or if you travel even a little.

We moved to Chicago, but we still own a house in Grand

Rapids. If I needed more things to wake me up in the night, there's one: the fact that all the equity we've built in ten years of home ownership is just sitting there in good old Grand Rapids, shrinking away, day by day. My neck literally hurts just thinking about it.

I was telling someone in Chicago about this recently, and he said, "Well, I know it's not what you planned, but now you have somewhere to stay if you want to spend some time on the lake. I hear the Michigan side of the lake is just beautiful."

First, do I look like I'm printing money? Does now seem like a good time for me to be thinking about a vacation place? And second, may I interest you in a map? Grand Rapids is thirty miles from the lake, making our home there, quite possibly, the worst lake house ever.

Between the war and the economy, we're receiving a steady stream of reasons to despair. I don't know the first thing about economics, but for the first time in my life, I find myself saying things like, "What happened to the Dow today?" I don't even know what the Dow really is, and what exactly it means when something happens to it, but I feel like I should ask.

I got a letter recently from our bank. Enclosed was a lovely little story, possibly written by a child, about rain and umbrellas and waiting out a storm, and essentially, it was a two-page way of saying, hey, don't freak out. Um, I wasn't, really, till my bank sent me a letter about storms and floods written either for or by a seven-year-old.

Deep breath. We are where we are. The world is as beautiful and broken as it ever was, and if you're anything like me, it takes some tricks to get back to centered, whole, deep-breathing, faith-filled places. On the days when, after watching the news or opening a letter from our bank, I'm tempted to lie down on the ground and let the anxiety I feel about our world flatten me like a steamroller, instead I do these things:

I pray. I speak to God, sometimes out loud, often in the car, frequently in the shower. I ask for help about things I don't understand. I ask for peace, and grace, and the ability to see outside myself. I pray for people who are at the mercy of these scary headlines—auto workers by the thousands who are losing jobs, children whose parents are unable to provide for them. And I pray for the people who can solve these problems— politicians both federal and local, pastors, philanthropists. I pray for a way through, a light at the end of the tunnel.

My friend Sarah, when her house in Grand Rapids was for sale, prayed every day for the family that would buy their home, for their health and safety, for any children who would be born in that home. She prayed for the exact right family, to bring light and hope and significant connections in the neighborhood. I thought this was very nice of her.

Meanwhile, my prayers sounded more like this: Dear God, please let somebody buy our house. Please let it be someone who's preapproved. I don't care if they bulldoze the house on the day of the closing or turn it into a meth lab or start raising livestock in the yard. I don't care if they're stockpiling weapons or if they have sixty-seven unspayed cats. I don't care if they're into midnight drum circles in the driveway or if they launder money in the basement. Just let them have good credit.

There is, however, a moral to this story. Sarah's house sold, and mine has not, and so now I have begun to pray for more than just solid financing. I pray for the things that will happen in that home, for the new family that will, someday, make their lives there. I pray for children who might be born in that home, remembering the moment we brought Henry home from the hospital to that very house. I pray for the way a new family will add to the lives of our neighbors, for Becky and Claudia and Katie and their families. I even try to find a reason that it's taken this long—maybe they're not ready to move, this family I'm praying for. Maybe there's something I can't see. And that's the core of prayer: admitting that just maybe, there's something going on that we can't see. So when I'm afraid, I pray, and I ask for God's help, that I will be able to see something I wasn't able to see before, or at least trust him to do the seeing.

Someone asked my dad recently how often we can pray for the very same thing, and he said that we should pray as often as we need to until the anxiety subsides, until, as it says in the Bible, we are filled with the peace that passes human understanding. That sounds delicious: peace that passes human understanding. That's what I'm starving for, and so I've been praying, sometimes even just the same phrase or sentence over and over again. I find that's an awful lot of praying for the same thing, but also that the anxiety does eventually subside, and the peace does indeed come, and it's pretty much the best feeling in the world.

Another thing, I find, that brings me a little peace is this: I try to help. In whatever ways, big or small, that I can, I try to help. When we moved in January, my friend Jamie called. She said, "I've been thinking about your move, and when I find myself thinking about someone, over and over, if I can't get them out of my head, I cook for them. When can I bring over dinner?"

She brought her super-famous chicken soup with bread and salad, lemonade and chocolate chip cookies, and if you've ever moved, you know what a gift it is to have someone feed you, when your pots and pans are in one of forty boxes marked "kitchen." And if you're anything like me, you start off with boxes that say, for example, *mixing bowls comma kitchen*, and by the end, your boxes say things like *winter coats, birdhouse, Pull-Ups, silver, etc.* In that moment, Jamie helped me more than she'll ever know. And I think, when you're worried, when you're overwhelmed, when it all seems like too much, it really helps to do something, even something small. Buy groceries for one person in your life who could really use them. Offer to babysit for new parents. Bring someone flowers. Do something.

Sometimes it helps to get outside our problems and stick our fingers into someone else's problems for a while. I volunteer sometimes at our church's food pantry, and often I show up, distracted and stressed, worried that I don't really have the time away from my computer to do this, that I'll fall behind, that I'll never make any writing progress if I keep using writing time to do other stuff. And then I sit across the table from a woman holding a baby, and we talk about her family. We walk together through the pantry, picking out fruit and meat and bread. I walk her to her car and help load the groceries in the trunk. As I leave, I know that I didn't solve her problems, by any means, but that for a few weeks, her cupboards will be full, and I was a tiny part of bringing that about. When so much feels out of control, that's something.

And finally, when it seems like there's more bad news than good, I gather the people I love around me. And sometimes that's the one that really helps. Sometimes what it takes for me to really regain a sense of God's hand and presence is nothing more than to stop the dozens of things I'm doing all at the same time and connect with my son. Everything stops in those moments when I finally stop trying to write one more email or put away a few more dishes or wrestle him into or out of the car seat one more time, and I really see him. I see the way his mind works and the way he sees the world, and I realize, in those moments, that the world he sees is full of beauty and mystery, that it's waiting to be discovered, new every day.

When I watch him, I realize that the Dow doesn't have nearly as much to say to me as this little person does, and it has very little bearing on the things that really matter, like our sons and daughters and the stories we write with them in our own homes every day. Those stories might not make for salacious headlines, but they do make beautiful lullabies, so sometimes the very best thing to do, I find, is to turn off the news and keep writing our own stories and lullabies.

twenty-two

SAN JUAN

This spring we went to San Juan because some dear South Haven friends asked me to officiate their wedding. Emily and Ryan are just absolutely extraordinary people, the kind of people you want to be around all the time. They're funny and smart, and they love their friends and family well, with tenderness and thoughtfulness. Being a part of their extended family and friends in San Juan felt like a gift, and being a part of their wedding was an honor.

The afternoon in Old San Juan was hot and clear and perfect, and I could hear the music of heels clacking along the black and white courtyard floors of the four-hundred-year-old convent. The twinkling lights in the low trees made it seem like we were in our very own universe, just for a little while. Emily was an absolute knockout bride, and her bridesmaids, elegant in black with bright, lovely flowers, laughed and cried as they celebrated their dear friend's marriage to Ryan, cool and charming as ever in his linen suit. My brother and the other groomsmen cheered Ryan on, thrilled to see the happiness on his face as Emily walked down the aisle.

During the ceremony, we incorporated a few Catholic traditions and a few Jewish ones, representing both their families and faiths. Sometimes those traditions seem old and distant, but in those moments they seemed fresh and infused with love and ocean air and the faces of the wedding party.

I had a deep sense that we were in the presence of something holy. Weddings are almost like birth experiences: something entirely new and sacred coming to life right in your midst. Of all the things I get to do, officiating weddings for people I love is my absolute favorite, because it's like being in the front row of the best show you've ever seen, or like being a midwife, but with no blood or screaming. When you officiate a wedding, you're right there in the moment of *before* and *after*, of single and married, of independent and "till death do us part."

For Ryan and Emily's wedding, I worked hard to get every word right, to capture their personalities and religious histories and family traditions. I wanted to honor them and use the very best language to express something about who they are and what matters to them, and how we, their friends and family, have been touched by them. On the day of the ceremony, all morning I prayed for them and thought about them. I wrote and rewrote my words for them by hand on hotel stationery.

It's so easy, when your own world feels a little dark and fragmented, to become increasingly self-focused, only able to see the frustration and pain of your own life. I brought my frustrated, wound-up self to San Juan and realized all at once that I was in the middle of something extraordinary.

Life hands us opportunities at every turn to get over ourselves, to get outside ourselves, to wake up from our own bad dreams and realize that really lovely things are happening all the time. Ryan and Emily were becoming a family, right there under the twinkling lights, and the beauty and meaning of that allowed me to lay down my sadness for a while.

I believe in the way God knits two people together when they stand before him on their wedding day. Something sacred happens in that moment, something that will, with grace and intention and faith and hard work, build upon itself and grow in power and beauty and durability with each passing year.

The ritual of a wedding is so beautiful and significant. Rituals allow us to connect to something we can't connect with in our daily, self-absorbed lives. Ryan and Emily's wedding put me back in the right direction, reminding me that it's not all about me, that love matters more than almost anything, and that when someone's life is changing, you better get over yourself and be present to the miracle in front of you.

I know a lot of people who have given up on marriage. I understand their objections. And I wish those people could have been in Old San Juan that day. I wish they could have felt the actual sensation of a new family being made. I wish they could have seen the bridesmaids' faces and heard Emily's Aunt Cheeps reading the Prayers of the Faithful. I wish they could have heard the loud crackle of the breaking of the glass and the cheers that rose up around Ryan and Emily during that beautiful Jewish tradition. There were, at some points in the ceremony, a few short moments of total silence, and in that silence what I felt was a community of friends and family who were all feeling the exact same thing at the exact same moment: *This matters. What we're creating here matters.* I believe in marriage, and possibly never more so than on that day.

After the ceremony we ate paella and beef tenderloin and spicy potatoes. We danced and drank mojitos. It was, without question, the dancing-est wedding reception I've ever been to: old people, small children, servers, band members, tambourines, bridesmaids, dance-offs. At one point, the darling bride was dancing to "Livin' on a Prayer" with one of the servers, while the father of the groom shook the tambourine over his head as he slid on his knees across the dance floor. The groom, not a dancer, surprised us with the worm, and the bandleader gave salsa lessons. There was, I believe, an air guitar-related injury in the bridal party at one point, and Grammie and Papaw, Emily's grandparents, stayed out on the dance floor longer than almost anyone, fox-trotting back and forth.

Maybe it was the dancing, or the black bean soup, or the navy blue cobblestones of Old San Juan. Maybe it was the warm, buttery mallorcas that Ryan brought to Aaron and me at the reception, ever the gracious host. Maybe it was the smell of the salt water or the sound of Emily's laughter. What I do know is that I'll always remember San Juan, and the feeling of being in the right place at the right time to actually watch the world become a little bit more beautiful.

twenty-three

THE TABLE

We were playing one of those games you make up on long flights to pass the time after you've finished all your magazines. My dad asked me about my favorite material possessions, the ones that mean the most to me, the ones I'd try to save in a fire. (Incidentally, since then, my brother's house burned down, so that's not something we bring up in casual conversation anymore.) I came up with three: the first, my wedding rings, both because of the sentimental value and because I think they're beautiful—antique-y and modern at once, both delicate and solid, symbols of the love story of our lives.

The second, also both sentimental and actual: my favorite purse. Right after I found out I was pregnant with Henry, I went to visit my dad in Europe for a long weekend while he was in the middle of a six-week trip. I used to travel with him a lot, but less so in recent years because of my own work schedule. I met him in Basel, Switzerland, a beautiful medieval

town, cobblestoned and bisected by a river, snowdusted. We
ran into a shop to get out of the swirling snow, and he bought
me a purse, made by a French designer I'd loved for years.
I love the purse, and I love the memories I carry within it.

And the third one is my table, once again for both reasons.
Our dining room table is almost ten feet long and four feet
wide, and if we snuggle, we can fit fourteen around it. It's
incredibly heavy, a rich reddish brown, rough, with a deep
scratch like a scar on a belly running down the center of it.
I bought it for a third of the original price, because of that scar,
and actually, I bought two, right then, similarly scarred. After
I'd bought them, I called my mom and asked her if I could keep
something in her garage, and also if she'd like a table. She said
yes to both. Aaron and I lived in a one-bedroom townhouse
without a dining room at the time, so my table lived in her
garage for over a year, and when we moved to Grand Rapids
and then back to Chicago, one of the criteria for both houses
was that they had to have room for our massive dining room
table, scarred and lovely.

The table matters to me because of what happens around
it. Nothing heals me or gives me life the way having people I
love around our table does. We've spent thousands of hours
at that table. Both our extended families have gathered there.
Henry had his first bite of baby food sitting on the table in a
bright blue Bumbo chair, and his first bite of cake in his high
chair there, carrot cake from Bar Louie on his first birthday,
an unseasonably hot October afternoon. After everyone else is
sleeping on dark December nights, I wrap Christmas presents
on it, one of my favorite parts of the holiday.

We've had fancy parties and entirely last-minute ones, big

parties and quiet dinners. When Annette and Andrew came to visit Grand Rapids for the first time, before they moved there, they arrived in the middle of a dinner party. We filled their plates and wineglasses and introduced them to our other guests. They moved to Grand Rapids shortly after, and the rest, as they say, is history. We've had parties for out-of-town friends, from Charleston and Philadelphia and Minneapolis and Orange County, and we've had low-key dinners with best friends hundreds of times, enough times that those evenings have a rhythm of their own, a sense of fluidity and familiarity, a sense of family.

If pressed, I'd say that risotto might be the meal most often served at our table. Enchiladas and lasagna, possibly, are runners-up. The enchiladas are Annette's recipe, or actually her sister Tina's, and the lasagna I most often make is Sara's, which is actually Martha Stewart's, I think. Spinach salad, certainly, warm whole grain bread wrapped in a towel, and brown rice. Salt and pepper shakers that Abby and Amy bought me, silver and weighty, classic. Lots of guacamole and a serious amount of pizza.

Aaron and I went through a pad thai season, and a pasta with pink sauce era, and an enduring quesadilla phase. For a while I made stuffing and green bean casserole with crunchy French fried onions all year round. We keep coming back to garlicky shrimp, roasted sweet potatoes, and a barbecue ranch chopped chicken salad my cousin refashioned from the take-out menu at the California Pizza Kitchen.

Henry has learned to eat at that table, and so far as we can tell, what he loves most is salsa—he uses the chips as spoons to transport the salsa to his little mouth, and if we let him he'll scoop it out of the bowl with his hands. He loves oranges, although he calls them apples, and he loves cheese—certainly his mother's son. He adores popcorn. He likes black beans, especially if they have a little salsa on them, and scrambled eggs. We went through a little stretch when all he wanted in the world was eggs! eggs! eggs!

Henry also loves peanut butter and jelly—a habit I think he picked up from my mother. He's not wild about olives at this point, but he does like hummus, risotto, steak, and peas. Also pizza, but who doesn't? If I had to live on only one food forever, certainly it would be pizza. Super thin crust pizza, with just cheese, or possibly fresh tomatoes, lots of salt, and a glass of champagne. Nothing better in the world, in my book.

When I lie awake at night and think about our life, these past few years have been without question the hardest of my life, and we're not through them yet. There have been a thousand tears, a thousand questions that still aren't answered. I don't know where our future is leading us, and I'm exhausted from trying to figure it out. Many of the assumptions I had made about life and faith and friendship shattered with some violence, and on many days it felt like the earth was moving beneath us and solid ground was a thing of the past. We felt untethered, like a space station that NASA forgot, and some days we could hardly stay awake past Henry's bedtime, because it was so exhausting to just push through the days.

But there are other things that I will remember, too, and that I think about over and over, like working a loose tooth with your tongue. There were meals: roasted chicken with kale and white wine on a blanket in Kirsten's backyard, spicy saag paneer and pappadams in the quiet of Jon and Christina's living room, homemade pizza at Alan and Sara's. I remember roasted red pepper and tomato soup at Ruth's and ham and potatoes at my grandmother's and risotto and lasagna and curry at our lovely, scarred table.

In the midst of what felt like a raging storm, we always came back to the table. The people we love met us there, and those moments were the ones that sustained us, literally and otherwise. In a season of melancholy and yearning, God met us in all sorts of places, in prayer and music and on the water and in our dreams and in his Word and in the voices of people we walk with, and certainly, graciously, he met us at the table.

twenty-four

EIGHT FOR EIGHT

I have seven dear friends from high school. We went to Barrington High School, famous for pot smoking, strong standardized test scores, and kids who drove Mercedes to school. We are now almost fifteen years from our high school graduation, and we see each other every year or so for an official gathering, and more often when life allows, dinners out and playdates.

For our most recent gathering, we spent a weekend at Ginger's new house in Chicago. After everyone arrived, after hugs and wine and dragging rolling suitcases all over the house, we walked in the cold November evening to Zia's, an Italian restaurant in Ginger's neighborhood, and sat at a round table filled with platters of pasta and bruschetta, our faces lit by candlelight, cheeks flushed from the cold. When we're together, we do what old friends do: we talk about the past we share and fill each other in on the daily present we no longer share. These women's faces hold oceans of memories for me, stories no one else would ever believe. They're like adolescent time capsules, lives lived long ago, and they're also sounding boards and fellow travelers in similar phases of life.

We're a funny mix, markedly similar in some ways and completely different in others—we are Italian, Irish, Polish, Dutch, but we're all kind of high-strung, get-it-done achievers. For context, we finally decided officially that *I'm* the laid-back one. My husband shuddered when he heard that, although he knows the girls well enough to know it's true. He said it almost makes him lose consciousness to contemplate the reality that there are several women on the planet more opinionated and fussy and intense than I am.

We went to eight different colleges, and now we do all kinds of work—among us an auditor, a journalist, a triathlete, a therapist. Seven of us have married over the last ten years, in weddings as different and similar as we are. One wedding on a Mexican beach, one castle in Ireland, one lovely Southern celebration, and a couple beautiful Catholic masses in beautiful Chicago churches. One is single, which is not what she would have chosen for her life at this point, a sensitive, tender reality she shares with us in quieter moments.

And in recent years, motherhood has descended upon several of us, with all the hope and love and beauty our hearts can contain, and all the pain and fear our souls can bear.

Five years ago, Elsa and Marc were the first to have children, and their lovely Italian baby girl was born on St. Patrick's Day. Is there anything more quintessentially Chicago than an Italian girl born on an Irish saint's holiday? When Elsa gave birth to her daughter, Isabella, what began as a beautiful birth experience became a medical emergency in the course of five minutes. Mother and daughter both were fine, eventually, but a hard delivery and high jaundice levels made for a fearful entry into motherhood.

Mary and Claire both struggled to get pregnant, and both endured months of heartbreak and mainstream and alternative approaches. They changed their diets, saw doctors, took medication, saw specialists. Now they're both mothers to darling babies, Abby and Benjamin, respectively, but none of us have forgotten the razor sharp pain of those months as they passed, especially as a few of us were pregnant right at the same time, bellies growing almost disrespectfully before their eyes.

Ginger's daughter, Samantha, was born with a rare chronic lung disease. The first years of her life have been characterized by terrifying trips to the hospital, to specialists, to foundations, a fight to get answers and help. Samantha is on continuous oxygen, and during flu season, for nine months throughout the Chicago fall, winter, and spring, Ginger and Samantha stay home. The only time they leave is for hospital visits. Samantha is charming and beautiful and tough and talks a mile a minute, but at the same time, the fear they live with all the time, under everything, is exhausting.

Courtney's youngest daughter, Mary Clare, is in the NICU as I write. Aidan is four and Callie is two, and every day, Courtney and Mark leave them with friends or family to visit MC, to talk to her and stroke her perfect baby skin and get updates from the doctors. She was born six weeks early, at just over three and a half pounds. She's doing better every day, but every mother who leaves the hospital without her baby knows how wrenching that moment is, how deeply wrong it feels. Courtney and Mark don't know the full extent of her challenges at this point, and are searching every day for signs of health and development.

Wendy doesn't know if she wants to have children, for all sorts of reasons. We talk about it together, and I respect her questions. I understand the pressure she feels to have children even though she's not sure it's what she and her husband want. So much of life, it seems, is about having the courage to ask your own questions instead of going with the script. The *get-married, have-babies* script is only best for some of us, even though so many voices tell us it's for everyone. I love that Wendy and Gary are walking their own path, on their own timing.

And I had a miscarriage not long after several of us had gotten together for a wild playdate, five of us, seven kids under four, three of us pregnant.

When I told Jenny I was pregnant this time, she texted back immediately that she was so happy for me, and that she wished she were pregnant, too. The honesty of that moment sliced me. I know she does, and I don't know why she hasn't yet found a person that's right for her to make a family with. Any man would be beyond lucky to make a family with her. When I talk with Jenny about it, I hear the deep yearning for something that hasn't yet come to be. We've all felt it, as different as our stories are.

In my most blind moments, I think that women without children live luxurious, carefree lives, filled with nothing but cosmopolitans, bikinis, and well-maintained highlights. I find that the phrase "She's let herself go" fills me with terror and guilt and panic as I look down at my jagged, dirty fingernails and overly soft tummy. I am she, certainly. And then I realize that as much as I want my friend Jenny's abs, she wants a baby, and we're all yearning for something.

When I take a step back, I'm surprised to realize that the topic of pregnancy and birth and mothering, for every single one of us, has been touched with pain or just a shade of heartache. The odds of that surprise me. Eight women, and eight stories of waiting or yearning, of brokenness mixed in with deep delight. If we're a microcosm, is this how it is? We're eight normal women, if normal even exists in this or any realm. And one by one, eight for eight, one or another aspect of motherhood has pricked us and made us bleed.

After the doctor's appointment that confirmed my miscarriage, one of the first things Aaron said was, "This is why it's so much easier not to love anything, because then your heart can never get broken." And it's true. If you open yourself to love, you open yourself to heartbreak. That's the nature of it.

As for my dear friends and me, our hearts are full, of course, but also a little tender, bruised, tired. Motherhood, and the journey toward it, has battered us a little bit, each in our own ways. From ambivalence to longing to loss, from the anger that our bodies won't do what we want them to, to the consuming, crushing love for a baby that is just hanging on. From the emptiness every month, over and over, to the physical brokenness of our bodies, to the deep questions— *When? When? When? Why? Why not?*

Motherhood has rumbled over us like a freight train, rendering us in some moments out of control and humbled, positions we're not accustomed to. We're get-it-done women. We've handled everything, all the time, all at the same time.

We've made lists and plans and back-up plans. And mother-hood laughed at our plans, twisted up our expectations, and gave them back to us upside down, covered with blood and stretch marks and Goldfish cracker paste.

Logic says mothers are crazy to hope as heedlessly as we do, to love as rabidly as we do, to care as recklessly as we do, to yearn as acutely as we do, but there's no other way. We have been made vulnerable by motherhood as we have by nothing else in our lives.

We are very thankful, of course, and we adore our children and one another's children. But as much as it's beautiful, the process is a little harrowing. Who knew we could want something so badly and then not be able to just wrestle it into existence? Who knew we could want to provide something so desperately for our children, to heal and protect them, but find ourselves profoundly unable? The stakes have gone up in our lives, the way they do, it seems, every time you decide to love something.

twenty-five

A BLESSING FOR
A BRIDE

For Emily and Christel in January,
for Kristin in February,
for Alli in July,
for Stacey and Lindsay in August,
for Laura, Emily, and Jenny in September,
for Paige and Laura in October,
and for Kristen in December.

People refer to your wedding day as the best day of your life. I understand why entirely. I remember my wedding day so absolutely clearly. I remember putting on the veil, seeing Aaron's face for the first time, the heaviness of my dress as I walked down the aisle with my dad. I remember the taste of the champagne and the sound of the band. I remember dancing with Aaron as though it was last night, and it was nearly eight years ago.

This is the thing, though: When people tell you that your wedding day is the best day of your life, what it sort of sounds like they're saying is that it's all downhill after the wedding is over. So many pastors make it a point to tell you, right during the ceremony, that it's all fun and games while you're wearing the dress and holding the flowers, but that serious business starts when the dancing stops. That's true, in some ways. Marriage is a serious business, and there's a lot to marriage that you can't see from where you're standing in the front of a church, bridesmaids surrounding you.

Your wedding day will, of course, be an extraordinary day. But on that day, you cannot imagine the beautiful, life-altering, soul-shaping things ahead of you. This is just the beginning. I know you believe that you could not possibly love him more than you do right now. I understand that. I felt that. I was wrong. I'm not an expert on anything, and certainly not on marriage, but I'm here to tell you that what you feel on your wedding day is like dipping your toe in an ocean, and with every passing year, you swim farther and farther from the shore, unable, at a certain point, to see anything but water. This is just the beginning, and you can't imagine the love that will bloom between you over time.

You will cry together, laugh together, pray and dance and move furniture together. You will learn and unlearn things, make a home together, hurt each other's feelings without meaning to, and sometimes very much on purpose. You will learn over time that the heart of marriage is forgiveness. You will learn in the first six months how much forgiveness he requires, and then you will realize, in the six months after that, just how much forgiveness you yourself need.

A piece of practical advice: you will not sleep well the night before your wedding. It's pretty much a fact. Your mind will rattle and shake, full of bizarre fears. You fear that your dress will fall off. It will not. You fear that you did not, in fact, secure a caterer. You did. You will fear, with each passing hour of the night, that your face is puffing up like a sausage and the area under your eyes is becoming blacker than an eight ball. This is not true. You are young, and a good makeup artist can cover a multitude of sins. You can try a sleeping pill, but you may find that it is no match for the running of your mind. Wake up a bridesmaid or your mother, make some tea, and let them remind you about the important things: the florist will indeed show up, your crazy uncle probably will hit on your bridesmaids, but they'll play it off graciously, and most important, you are indeed ready to be a wife.

Don't worry too much about all the advice that other people are giving you, mine, of course, included. I remember getting my nails done the day before my wedding. All the ladies at the salon were wishing me luck and wanted to see my ring, and giving bits of sweet, innocuous, helpful advice like, "Make sure you eat a sandwich so you don't pass out during the ceremony," and, "Bring a piece of chalk to cover any marks you get on your dress before pictures." Thanks, ladies.

And then one woman says, "Whatever you do, don't have one of those weddings where they don't even give you any dinner. They call it heavy hors d'oeuvres, but my husband and I just starved!" Oh, heavens. That's exactly what we were having, heavy hors d'oeuvres. Ma'am, it's the day before my wedding. Do you think I'm just now considering catering options? Quick, let me call the caterer right now and change everything because one lady at the salon was hungry one time after a wedding.

Keep in mind that there are a million ways to do a wedding, and that for whatever reason, people feel extraordinarily free to comment on anything they feel is out of the ordinary. Consider this great training if you should one day decide to have children. Advice on cakes and seeing each other before the ceremony is a great warm-up for unsolicited lectures on the ills of epidurals, the importance of delayed vaccinations, and many varied ways you will probably damage and scar your precious new life.

Part of being a married couple means that you create a new identity together, woven from your experiences and histories and lives, and while the whole world is replete with opinions and recommendations, work hard to become your own family, with your own values and traditions, things you always do, things you never do, things that bring you back to why you fell in love in the first place. Dance to your song in the backyard, wear your wedding shoes every anniversary. Carve out your own history together, little by little, month by month, year by year. Because there will be seasons that are as dry as deserts, and the history of your love for one another will be the water you need to bring new life and growth, turning that season from dust to garden once again.

Today is about the promise of the future and all the great moments of the past and, indeed, this beautiful present where you stand together, surrounded by people who love you and who are praying that your marriage is one of the great ones. It could be, you know, if you work hard and forgive often, and get over yourself and your selfishness over and over again.

It could be one of the stories people tell, when they want to believe in love's power and life's richness. It could be one that your children and grandchildren tell each other, praying that someday they'll have a love like yours.

My grandparents celebrated their sixtieth wedding anniversary this year. They are one of those couples that are living a love story every day, even after sixty years. They went to third grade together, and then Grandma's family moved away. And when they met again at seventeen, Grandpa swears he remembered that beautiful face from the third grade. They were married at the Justice of the Peace, just before Grandpa left for the Navy. They moved to Hawaii a few years after the attack on Pearl Harbor, and Grandpa and his friends spent their days surfing on longboards while Grandma and the other women laid on the beach in Hawaiian-print bikinis.

Life took them to California for a few years, and then back home to Michigan. They sailed in the Caribbean and kept a sailboat in South Haven. At their house in Kalamazoo, Grandpa worked in his shop while Grandma tended her roses, all along the white fence. We watched them slow dance in the kitchen and loved to look through their pictures from Hawaii and their sailing trips. They love to ride bikes together, and for their seventy-fifth birthdays, they took their tandem recumbent bike to Washington, DC, to ride along the Potomac.

They're fairly certain that the movie *The Notebook* is a story about them, and I can see why. They have that thing, that romantic, connected thing that we all want, the reason we stand in front of churches and make vows before God and witnesses.

On the night of their anniversary party, we had dinner and cake and when we toasted them, essentially, we all said the same thing. We each said our own versions of *thank you for having a marriage that gives us something extraordinary to aspire to.* Thank you for all the times we caught you kissing in the kitchen and all the times you showed us pictures of your wedding and your years in Hawaii and your sailing trips and bike rides. Thank you for giving us a picture of how we could be, if we work really hard and are very good to one another. Thank you for living with so much love and tenderness and laughter that we have in you a real life picture of how good it can be.

You, my dear friend, will be a bride for one day, but you will, with God's grace and your own very hard work, be a wife to this man every day for the rest of your life. Being a bride is super-fun, but it pales in comparison to the thrill and beauty of being a part of one of the truly great partnerships, like my grandparents. Make your love story one worth telling. Make it one worth living, every day, as long as you both shall live.

twenty-six

LOVE SONG FOR FALL

Aaron and I took Henry for a walk in his wagon last week, and in the glow of late afternoon, we walked by a tree that had begun changing earlier than the rest. It felt like the very first moment of fall, we commented as we walked. And then on Sunday morning, I bought a bunch of pumpkin trees with tiny, perfect pumpkins, orange and green, on thick branches. Now there's fall in a vase on our dining room table. Later that day we went for a bike ride and got caught in a rainstorm, and the smell of dirt and the yellow of wildflowers against the gray sky were unmistakably fall.

I'm paying close attention to the change of seasons these days, because I need a change to move me forward, and I'll take anything I can get. Today I need to end a season of time wasting, fear, obsessive blog-reading, and totally nonessential Wikipedia research. First step: I met a friend at a coffee shop. I left the house a mess, choosing to believe that writing is, for this morning, more important than cleaning up toys. Writing is a mind game for me, and I'm not above some tricks to get me out of this terrible stuck place I've been for about six weeks, maybe longer.

I was on iTunes making a playlist the other day, looking for inspiration anywhere I could find it, and as I scrolled through all the options, I felt like I hadn't heard of practically any of the bands. And I thought to myself, how many bands *are* there? How many bands does the world need?

Yikes. That's the wrong question, the worst ever, most art-killing question there is. So much of life, really, comes down to asking the wrong questions. This is the thing about art: it's not about market demand. It's not like trying to figure out if this town needs another grocery store or dry cleaner. It's more like a million voices all yelling out one word over and over, and every once in a while the sound makes the whole world sit up straight and pay attention for a split second.

The world doesn't need another band, per se. It doesn't, strictly speaking, need another book or another photograph or another album. The general world population will survive without one more stage production and one more gallery showing.

This is the thing, though: you might not. We create because we were made to create, having been made in the image of God, whose first role was Creator. He was and is a million different things, but in the beginning, he was a creator. That means something for us, I think. We were made to be the things that he is: forgivers, redeemers, second chance-givers, truth-tellers, hope-bringers. And we were certainly, absolutely, made to be creators.

If you were made to create, you won't feel whole and

healthy and alive until you do. My husband is a pianist and songwriter, and you can set a timer by his need to play and create. If it's been too long, I can feel it in our house, like something gone bad in the refrigerator or a dead mouse in the walls. He was made to play, to sing, to create with sounds and notes and words, and when he doesn't, he's not himself.

I know there are some artists who create around the clock, who feel art coursing through their very veins, who can go without sleep and food and human interaction for days while they revel in the rich universe of their own minds. But I think those artists are very rare, or maybe that they're fibbing. I think for most of us, it's hard work, fraught with fear and self-consciousness, and that it's much easier to make dinner or mow the lawn or reply to emails.

Today as I write I'm sitting with my friend Margaret, a screenwriter. We're not talking, mostly, but we're doing the most important work one artist can do for another: we're keeping each other in the chair and off the internet. I can keep working if she can, and she can keep working if I can. Some days it all comes down to tricks and discipline.

We make art by putting the time for it on the calendar with all the glamour of scheduling a dental cleaning. We sit down and work. We pray and stare out the window and force ourselves to keep typing. We stay in our chairs and fight the urge to fold the laundry, desperate for something to control, something orderly and safe instead of the wild, untamed world of our own secret feelings and imaginations.

And we do it because it makes us feel aware and alive and created for a purpose more than almost anything else in our lives. There are a zillion things I don't do well, a thousand things I do just because I'm human and I have to, and when I do them I certainly don't feel any spark of having been created for something very specific and tender. I don't feel anything when I do the dishes or when I drive or when I buy groceries.

But every once in a while, when I write, I feel that feeling of a thousand slender threads coming together, strands of who I've been and who I'm becoming, the long moments at the computer and the tiny bits of courage, the middle of the night prayers and the exact way God made me, not wrong or right, just me. I feel like I'm doing what I came to do, in the biggest sense. That's why I write, because sometimes, every once in a while, I feel entirely at home in the universe, a welcome and wonderful feeling. I could cry at that feeling, because it happens so rarely. Doing the hard work of writing makes me feel like I'm paying my rent on a cosmic level, doing the thing that I can do to make the world a little better decorated. Writing wakes me up, lights me on fire, opens my eyes to the things I can never see and feel when I'm hiding under the covers, cowering and consumed with my own failures and fears.

Fall in Chicago is an event. It's like theater: active, kinetic, rich. Fall is harvest, when we're getting all the good stuff that someone took the time to plant many months ago. Someone planted it, and now we benefit from it. And that's how it is when we make art. We struggle and push and plant seeds deep underground, and it doesn't look like much for a while. But then someone comes along and listens to your song or sees your painting or reads your poem, and they feel alive again, like the world is fresh and bursting, just like harvest. Plant something today that will feed someone many months or many years from now. Plant something today, because you've feasted on someone else's carefully planted seeds, seeds that bloomed into nourishment and kept you alive and wide-eyed.

Use what you have, use what the world gives you. Use the first day of fall: bright flame before winter's deadness; harvest; orange, gold, amber; cool nights and the smell of fire. Our tree-lined streets are set ablaze, our kitchens filled with the smells of nostalgia: apples bubbling into sauce, roasting squash, cinnamon, nutmeg, cider, warmth itself. The leaves as they spark into wild color just before they die are the world's oldest performance art, and everything we see is celebrating one last violently hued hurrah before the black and white and silence of winter. Fall is begging for us to dance and sing and write with just the same drama and blaze.

Use your dreams and your secrets and your neglected, hidden imagination. Write a love song for someone who will never love you back. Write a comedy that used to be a tragedy, because you can create any ending you want for your own story. Write a song that says everything you've ever wanted to say to your father, or fill a canvas with all the things you hope you find out that God is, when you meet him someday. Dance till your feet bleed, sing till you're hoarse, spill out all your stories like pouring wine into thin-stemmed glasses, the liquid rich and blood-red.

Get up. Create like you're training for a marathon, methodically, day by day. Learn your tricks, find a friend, leave the dirty dishes in the sink for a while. This is your chance to become what you believe deep in your secret heart you might be. You are an artist, a guide, a prophet. You are a storyteller, a visionary, the Pied Piper himself. Do the work, learn the skills, and make art, because of what the act of creation will create in you.

twenty-seven

RAVENOUS

I think I may have a larger appetite than most people. I mean that in terms of food, certainly, and in terms of absolutely everything else, too: I want more food, more time, more people, more places, more parties, more everything. *More* is a big theme in my life. Other themes in the same vein: hungry, insatiable, and gluttonous. I'm pretty certain that I could out-eat most women my size, should the opportunity ever present itself. Sometimes I see tiny women on TV eating like fifty-eight hot dogs, and I think to myself, *Please, I could eat a hundred of those.* I did hold the record for most ice cream sandwiches at my summer camp: eleven and a half.

Aaron loves to bet people money that they can't eat crazy portions or combinations of food, but he never bets me. First, because I'll take him up on it every time, and second, because we share money, which makes it a little less exciting. On vacation one year, he bet my brother a hundred dollars to drink thirty ounces of prune juice with pulp, and we have an absolutely fabulous photo of Todd, having recently vomited, with a bloody nose and red-rimmed eyes, holding an empty bottle of prune juice in one hand and a hundred dollar bill in the other. My mother was furious, but the rest of us laughed till we cried.

I'm ravenous in all sorts of other ways, too. I'd like to host a dinner party about every other day. I think life is delicious, and I want to gobble it up in big bites, eating, drinking, reading, talking, traveling—everything. I want everything. I'm hungry for everything, all the time. Bookstores make me ravenous, as do city streets and airports and glossy fashion magazines. So much to see, taste, touch, try, do. I can feel myself come to life, eyes open, taking everything in, fingers running over textures, ears pricked for sounds. I feel like life is so genuinely interesting, that there's so much to be tasted and tried and discovered.

I love it when a day's activities stack up on top of each other perfectly, from breakfast to work to lunch to grocery shopping to coffee, all the way through till I fall into bed. I love days when you're always leaving something early to arrive just a touch late at the next place, like pearls on a string or Tarzan swinging on vines, feet never touching the ground.

Or really, I love the idea of that way of living, so I sign myself up for it every chance I get. And then I realize in the moment that it isn't what I wanted at all. After a while, I'm frantic and tired and not really listening when people are talking. I'm frazzled and frustrated that Henry doesn't want to get in the car again, but of course he doesn't. Why would he want to get dragged around on the crazy whirlwind that I think will keep me happy?

I've been around this block a thousand times. I'm ravenous,

and life looks to me so sparkly and beautiful, waiting to be devoured like a perfect apple. So I say yes, yes to everything, to that meal and that event and that trip and that person. It's so delicious, and I don't want to miss out on even one moment of it. And that's the point: I miss all sorts of sacred and significant moments, because of my frantic insistence that I can do it all, and that I don't have to miss anything. I run from thing to thing, and then I fall into bed at night without even the space to think about the day. I wake up again to start it all over: more people, more food, more play, more ideas, more books. I'm ravenous, and somewhere along the way what started as a clean and lovely lust for life crosses over into a cycle of frantic activity, without soul or connection. I'm surprised every time. How did I get here again? Don't I know better than this?

I'm looking a little deeper these days at this feeling: where did it come from? What's it about? Is there something better than *more*? I think that our deepest darknesses are always the other side of the coin of our brightest selves. I think exuberance and celebration are wonderful things, and I'm thankful for the ways that they play out in my life. But there's a darkness under that shimmer, and it keeps me exhausted and running, year after year, always thinking that maybe this time, maybe this time, I can fit it all in, and nothing will fall through my fingers.

And now it's December again, and being me in December is like being an alcoholic in a bar: temptations abound. In other months, I spend a lot of my time cooking up fun things to do—parties, trips, shopping lists. But December, lovely month, does it all for me. It's all my favorite things coming together—special occasions, traditions, gatherings centered around food and presents. We're not even halfway through the month, and the damage is done. A weekend in the city, a party tonight, a night out tomorrow. Birthday parties and Christmas parties and cookie exchanges and dinners. And just like every time, I slip into believing that more is more, that if one dinner party is good, two is better, that if one caramel is good, four is much better, that if staying up to read for an hour is good, then all night is even better.

But I keep coming back to the old cliché, less is more. Coco Chanel, the queen of all chic, famously said that before you leave the house, you should remove one item. Not like your pants. Like a necklace or a scarf or something. I'm pretty good about this from a fashion standpoint. I feel like I have one of those faces where there's a lot going on, so I never wear earrings. But in my life, I'm a *more is more* girl, and I'm struggling to make the change.

I want to really notice each meal, each bite, each conversation, instead of shoving food in my mouth, running out the door, promising someone we'll connect again soon. I can always tell I'm on thin ice when my list of promises becomes way too long. I have so many intentions and plans, but I lose the ability to listen, to stay, to connect. I'm embarrassed that I fall for it every time, that even this month I've been more ravenous and gluttonous than I'm proud of. *Less is more* is a great idea, but you wouldn't know that from my calendar.

We all have a kooky set of fears and loves that makes us do what we do. For me, I love experiences, and it makes me scared to think of missing out on anything at all. So that fear drives me and takes over my life, pushing me to do more, buy more, eat more, try more. But I don't want to be ruled by fears. There will be more life to experience tomorrow. And the next day, and the next day. And I don't have to be running after it all the time. Breathe, rest, practice the idea of enough. Practice the idea of living well, and a little more slowly. Practice believing that it will all still be here, waiting to be devoured freshly, after a good night's sleep.

When I was single, I was a little more cavalier about all this. I'm not hurting anyone. I just like to play, right? Of course I was hurting myself, compromising my best life, and also hurting people I made empty promises to and people I raced past, too busy to connect or care. And now when I lose that balance, Aaron pays for it, and Henry pays for it. They watch me run out the front door, blowing kisses on my way out, promising I'll be home sooner than we all know is possible. Or they accompany me, and they get dragged from party to party, store to store, experience to experience, feeling distant and bedraggled. So this is no longer just my problem, as though it ever was. This is something I do to my family. That's why I mean business in a new way this time, because of that tiny little face, asking me to stay home, because of Aaron's tired eyes, asking when I'll be back. Less is more.

I don't know the way through to the other side on this one, but I do know that I don't want to be ruled by ravenous anymore, and that full life is not the same as a full calendar. Full life is lived when the whole system works together, when rest and home and peace live hand in hand with taste and sparkle and go. I've believed in the craziness for too many years, and while I still have a lot of questions, the answer I need to be giving most often these days is NO.

twenty-eight

WHOLE HEART

Henry, today you are three. Happy birthday, baby.

When I was pregnant, I prayed that you would be strong and happy. I know that there are probably better words to choose, but those are the ones that made sense to me, and so I prayed them over and over with my hands on my belly. And each year on your birthday, I am so incredibly thankful that those words describe you perfectly.

I remember when you were just beginning to stand, just for a moment. You looked at us, eyes glowing, knowing that you had struck upon something new and important. I remember so clearly those two front teeth, little white planks, like Tic Tacs or tiny white surfboards jutting up from your little horseshoe gum. Your smile and smell of your neck and the round gurgling sound of your laugh when I tickled your legs: those things are embedded in the deepest parts of me, like memory devices, like code, like magnets.

Your eyes have always been so *blue* blue, and when they're closed, your eyelashes make the most perfect fan of fine black lines, just the same as when you were a baby. New babies are so precious and clean, but a toddler boy is a filthy, stinky little darling. Baby or not, I still feel a physical ache for the smell of your head, not that perfectly sweet newborn scent anymore, but your own funny boy smell, distinctly like toast. When I'm not with you, all I want is to feel your little arms and legs wrap around me like a starfish.

I went to a baby shower earlier this week, and I remember the showers our friends threw before you were born. I remember being pregnant, wondering who you'd be. Henry, even in my best dreams, I never could have imagined you. My favorite people in the world have big, huge personalities and a little bit of swagger, and it brings me delight to no end that you have more swagger than almost anyone I know. People laugh when they meet you or when they see you walking through Trader Joe's, pushing your own little cart full of waffles and clementines. I think it's because you walk like a grown man, belly pushed out, arms swinging. You walk like you own the place wherever you go, a cross between a cowboy and Tony Soprano.

The two words that have always described you just exactly are *irrepressible* and *luscious*. Irrepressible, because you are a force, a wild animal, a ham. You act out elaborate stories and jump off the couch sixty times in a row, yelling, "To infinity and beyond!" each time. You are so physical, so rough and wiggling, and then in the very next moment, you want me to hold you like a baby, stroking my face with Lambie. And you are just luscious—round, pink cheeks, tender neck, grubby, chubby hands. Every part of you is round and grab-able and waiting to be kissed.

I feel like an adolescent boy on a date with a pretty girl when I'm with you, desperate to touch you, willing to concoct any ruse to get you to sit on my lap or let me kiss your neck. I remember from high school and college how almost everything an adolescent boy does is done with the goal of touching a girl—tickling, fake fighting, showing her how to shoot pool, showing her how to hold a golf club or a baseball bat or how to play a chord on the guitar, wrapping his arms around hers, fingers on fingers. Mostly, the girl doesn't notice, or plays along, and if I'm lucky, you don't notice, or you play along. I confess that I make up whole games just so I can smell that little place at the side of your neck, the place that smells just exactly like toast and sleeping.

I feel like I could eat you up. My fingers twitch with the ache to touch your skin, to scrape your fine hair across your sweaty moist forehead, to pat your little buns. Speaking of buns, the total appropriateness of the term "buns" makes sense to me now, now that I see your little buns as you cruise around, fresh from the bath, before we can wrestle you into your Batman underwear.

When you were two, when you got so tired and upset about something that you couldn't pull it together, you'd moan, "I want to be happy," through your tears and boogers. That seemed like such an honest, human thing to say. When we're tired and angry and teary, that's what we all want, right?

You are in a hardcore superhero phase. So long and so emphatic that "phase" might be the wrong word. At this point, it might be a lifestyle. Every day, I give you a choice between a few different superhero T-shirts, and you pick which cape, mask and belt you'd like to go with the shirt you've chosen. Don't tell anybody, but this summer at the lake, the only shirt you wore for twenty-eight days was your Superman shirt. I'd throw it in the wash with the beach towels every other day or so. You did go without a shirt about 50 percent of the time we were there, but I don't know if that makes it better or worse. Now we're smarter, and we have a bazillion superhero options, so that you always have a choice, even when I'm a little behind on the laundry.

Sometimes we lie down on the carpet in the living room, your arm hooked around my neck. You're Superman and I'm Lois Lane, and without your arm around me, I'd fall out of the sky, but you whisper, "Don't worry, Lois, I've got you."

You like to pray sometimes, but sometimes you don't want to. That makes me think you're fairly normal. Sometimes you pray fervently, grasping my hand in yours, making long lists of things you're thankful for, and other times you try to wink at people during the whole prayer. Since you can't wink, it's really just emphatic blinking, but I find it highly amusing in any case, and usually we both get in trouble for giggling.

You are absolutely fearless, and as a mom, I love this about you, and it worries me. You never think the water is too deep or the waves are too big or the jump down from the monkey bars is too far. It scares me because I think we'll spend a lot of time in the emergency room, but at the same time, I love this about you, kid. You're wide open all the time. You run everywhere you go, and even when you sleep, you're sprawled out, turned over, pink-cheeked. Boy after my own heart, of course. My parents tell me all the time that I deserved a kid like you. They tell me this when you're being naughty—when you run away from me, or when you look me in the eye and say no. They say, *you deserved this,* as they laugh.

But I know better than to think for even one second that I deserve you, Henry. You're all the best parts of life. You teach me and push me and wear me out, and you delight me and make me laugh so hard I cry. I don't know how I ended up with a kid like you, but I'm thankful every day.

You know this already, because I tell you every day, but I love you with my whole heart. When you were first born, and I was so totally overcome with the way I felt about you, that's what I whispered to you, and it's as true today as it ever was. I love you with my whole heart.

twenty-nine

JOIN THE CLUB

My last thought as I was falling asleep last night was a thankful prayer for our cooking club and for what we've become. We began meeting together once a month to cook. I knew each woman, but they didn't all know each other. We got together for the first time on Oscar night just after Aaron and I moved back to Chicago. That night we made updated comfort foods, and in between Oscar speeches, we ate macaroni with gruyère and fontina, and pecan sweet potato casserole, and turkey meatloaf sliders with white cheddar and spicy ketchup. I made introductions over dinner, telling my cousins how long Brannon and I have known each other, telling the Chicago girls how long Josilyn's family and mine have been spending summers together in South Haven.

We made tapas at Amanda's and brunch at Melody's and celebrated Cinco de Mayo with enchiladas and mango salsa at Josilyn's. We had lemon bundt cake and pork tenderloin over grilled creamed corn at Casey's, and bowl after bowl of soup around my table in the fall. In the summer, we cooked together at the blue house in South Haven. While we prepped vegetables and washed blueberries, we took turns watching the kids play on the porch.

Last night they all came over to make a cookbook, a record of our first year together. Henry and Emme played happily under the table while we ate thin slices of honeycrisp apples and leftover Halloween candy. We proofed recipes and downloaded photos and wondered aloud about the spelling of "prosciutto" and "avgolemono." We were tired and full of candy when we finally pressed *send*, and as I rinsed the teacups after they left, I thought about the last several months, and I realized that we've actually become that elusive thing that churches have been trying to create in small groups for decades: we've become a community.

We're not best friends, all of us. We have other best friends, sisters, other worlds. But the hours we spend around the table grow every month, and before and after we talk about food, we talk about our lives. We talk about food and family and speech therapists and what constitutes a good date. We talk about shoes and depression and kosher salt versus sea salt.

We stayed extra-long around Melody's table one cold night this fall as she told us about her third miscarriage since Marley's birth. We had eaten frittata and French toast strata, apple crumble and Florentine crepes, and we pushed our plates away as quietly as possible, none of us willing to get up from the table. I sat at one end of the table, and Melody sat at the other, and between us, the faces of all these people who cared about her, who wanted to carry this with her. Melody is my cousin, my oldest friend. We were born three weeks apart, slept over at each other's homes a few nights a week growing up, lived together after college, celebrated our children's births six weeks apart. Her sister and I were at the table, representatives of history and home and safety. But there were new friends around the table, too, and the love on those faces was a gift, both to her and to me that night.

I've been in what seems like a thousand groups that never really came together, and then just a very few that really did. And I'm learning a few things about both kinds of groups. First, I think a lot of groups, church-based or otherwise, fail because they can't find themselves under the weight of expectations placed upon them. Sometimes, with the best of intentions, when we start small groups or accountability groups or life groups, we saddle them with the idea that they have to be deeply intimate and transformational right at the first meeting. We force connections that aren't there, fumble through topics and conversations and routines that feel forced and hollow, and then we wonder why we don't actually want to go that often.

I was struck by a new wave of loneliness during our last season in Grand Rapids, even after several years there. I was traveling most of the time, and the time I did spend in town was largely at home with Henry and Aaron, writing, doing laundry, and making grocery lists. The town felt like a totally different place, like we ripped out the stitches of a garment, and now nothing held the whole together. And right in that time, my friend Steve invited me to join his book club.

I didn't expect them to meet my deepest needs, and I certainly didn't tell them that the reason I was joining had more to do with loneliness than a desire to read the classics.

The first night I was a little bit nervous. I was older than most of them, one of the only married ones, the only parent. They were hipsters who hate chain restaurants and have long conversations about brewing their own beer. I barely even drink beer.

Together we read the classics, the books we should have read in college but somehow didn't. We had animated discussions both about the books we read, but especially about the selection of next month's choice. We read *Madame Bovary*, and *Catch 22*, and *The Beautiful and the Damned*. We read *My Antonia* and *Slaughterhouse Five* and *For Whom the Bell Tolls*. It seemed that someone always brought hummus, either from Marie's or Pita House, and there was always chocolate and always red wine.

We didn't become best friends or share our deepest darkest secrets, but I looked forward to book club night all month long. Some of it was that book club reminded me of college, of being an English major, of the language and rhythm of people who love to talk about books. Book club was a chance to indulge my inner book-nerd, a chance to rediscover a part of myself and my history long-hidden.

I love the way a book connects people, even if some people loved it and some people hated it. Reading together means we entered the same story, we walked the same streets and witnessed the same deaths and weddings. It means whatever was different about our months—some were students, some traveled for business, some worked downtown—wherever we were, we were carrying around the same story, reading a few pages at a time, staying up late.

The books and the time we spent in each other's homes

connected us over time and made my life in that season feel richer. I think that's how it happens, most of the time, kind of by accident when you're doing something you love, and only when you're lonely enough to take a risk.

There have been a few times—two, to be specific—when I've been a part of an official small group that's really connected and become what a small group should be. I'm really thankful for the small group of girls I led when I worked in student ministry, and thankful as well for our housechurch in Grand Rapids. Both continue to teach and shape and anchor me. But I've been a part of a whole bunch of official groups that felt forced or awkward, where one person's expectations weighed down the whole, or it felt like a bad first date, or someone shut down every time things got a little honest. I know so many people who are just done with the whole official small group thing, and I understand why.

This is what I would say to them: find connection and community wherever it already is, even in tiny ways, in your life. Take a risk and cultivate the tiniest possibility of connection, even in the unlikeliest of places. Sometimes it does work to set out together for intimacy, honesty, truth-telling. But more often, in my experience, you find those things by going through the back door—serving together, cooking together, reading together.

I've watched my dad and my brother sail with the same team of sailors for almost twenty years. And when you see them on a boat together, it's amazing to watch—they anticipate each other's moves, communicate wordlessly, laugh uproariously when the same guy does the same thing he's been doing for twenty years. But the real magic is what happens after the boat is back at the dock. They've stood in one another's weddings, surrounded one another at funerals of family members, fielded middle of the night phone calls, and celebrated great accomplishments. They are, in a word, a community.

It doesn't happen overnight, and it doesn't happen the moment you decide to make the call or show up at the group. But I'm finding that it's there waiting for you in all sorts of unexpected places, that when you do what you love with people who love the same thing, something is born into your midst and begins to connect you. It might not be officially recognized, but then it doesn't need to be.

In a world that's wracked by loneliness and ravaged by divisions, those connections are no small thing. If they make you better, more honest, more loving, if the presence of Christ is apparent because of the way that you love each other, because of the good things you bring out in each other, then what else is it?

When you walk with someone, listen to their story, carry their burden, play with their kids, that's community. When you pray for them in the middle of the night because their face popped into your mind, when you find yourself learning from them and inviting them more and more often into the family places in your life, that's community, and wherever you find it, it's always a gift.

thirty

PRINCESS-FREE ZONE

Aaron and I went to Miami with Annette, Andrew, and Joe for a long weekend a few years ago. We had done extensive online research, and I believed that I had found the holy grail of South Beach hotels: a spacious suite with two bedrooms and a kitchen, free happy hour and breakfast, and all that right on Collins Avenue, in the center of everything, walking distance to the beach.

When we arrived, we found that it was indeed on Collins, and that it was in fact walking distance from the beach. However, the breakfast and happy hour were both truly awful, and the "two bedrooms and a kitchen" part was a flat-out lie: there were two queen beds in the main part of the room, and then across from the bathroom there was a futon, a mini-fridge, and a bookcase with a few cans of warm Coke—the "kitchen" and "second bedroom," we presumed.

We had also failed to realize that we were going to South

Beach right in the middle of spring break, and didn't know that they were filming an episode of *The* OC while we were there either. It was insanity, and we decided that the only sensible thing to do was to join in. We bought a cooler on wheels, made sangria with cheap red wine from the drugstore and fruit from our hotel's breakfast buffet, and set up at the beach, iPod speakers blaring.

On our first morning there, while the boys played catch in the water, Annette and I laid face down on our towels, listening to music, until we realized that someone was standing in our sun. We squinted up at a big man with a big camera, wearing a *Girls Gone Wild* hat. We had seen him before, because we had the good fortune to be staying at the same hotel as the entire *Girls Gone Wild* crew, and also approximately every sorority girl in the state of Florida.

He told us that if we went out in the water and kissed and took off our bikini tops while he was filming, he'd give us each a hat. We stared up at him, and then at each other, and then back at him. Where to start, really?

We interrupted each other a few times, sputtering out unrelated phrases like, "Um, those are our husbands, right there in the water . . ." and, "You know, that's not really our deal . . ." and, "Uh, we're like a lot older than you think we are . . ." Finally, we gave up explaining and said, "No, thank you. No. No, thank you."

He shuffled away, and a few minutes later, there were lots of girls in the water, kissing and taking their tops off, and then a minute after that, the girls were running back to their towels wearing their brand-new hats.

Huh. Questions abound. Our first question: "Wait—did he really think we were that young?" But then our second question: "Wait—did he really think we were that stupid?"

After we were done congratulating ourselves for momentarily passing as younger than we were, we were dumbfounded, and then a little angry. A hat? Seriously? You think that baring my breasts on television is only worth a hat? And just for conversation's sake, where, dear sir, am I going to wear that hat? On a job interview? To my grandma's house?

My friend Brannon has a darling little girl named Emmeline. Emme is as absolutely girly as they come—she loves to wear fancy dresses, she's delicate and sensitive and plays with babies. But before Emme was born, Chris and Brannon declared their house a princess-free zone. There could be pink, there could be dresses and lace and babies galore, but no tiaras, no wands, and no princes coming to rescue any little princesses.

I love this. I think maybe we should all live in a princess-free zone. I think the current cultural messaging that tells women it's attractive to play dumb and fragile and hope that they're saved by their beauty is incredibly destructive. And I don't consider men the only problem. Every woman who plays cute instead of smart, who is known for her body more than for her brains, or who depends on her pout to get what she wants is part of the problem.

Let me be clear: when it comes to little girls playing princess, I know that to a certain extent all bets are off. Before Henry was born, I felt very strongly that our child would never play with guns and never watch movies with any amount of violence. Now, at three, he can make a gun out of a crayon, a baby fork, or his own finger, and on a regular basis Batman saves the world from crashing, burning disaster on our TV screen while Henry watches in rapt attention. My husband assures me that there's hope, because he spent three solid years believing he was actually Rambo, killing left and right in his imaginary world, and he grew up to be a pacifist. I'm hoping that's true for our little gunslinger, and I do understand hard-wiring in a way that I didn't until I had Henry.

So if you're going to do the princess thing with your little girls, finding it as inevitable as we're finding superheroes and their weapons with our little boy, do it the way my friends Brian and Jorie do it: their three girls are as girly as you can imagine—shoes with glitter and flowers in their hair, capes and tiaras everywhere you look. At the very same time, though, they're tough and energetic and fearless. They love to wrestle with their dad, and those three firecrackers aren't waiting around to be saved by any princes. Frankly, if I'm ever in trouble, I hope one of Brian and Jorie's darling, tough princesses comes to save me.

And really, it's not the two-year-old princesses I'm worried about. They're in it for the fancy dresses, and I certainly understand the draw there. The princesses I'm worried about are the ones who are twenty-two, thirty-two, and forty-two, women who play fragile in order to be rescued at any age.

I'm not anti-feminine. I'm super-girly in lots of ways, and I operate, in many ways, within squarely traditional gender roles. I love to cook, I love fashion, and I don't feel demeaned at all refilling your drink. I like to do it, actually. I could talk your ear off about makeup and maternity fashion and what makes the perfect marinara. I hate to drive, am terrible with technology of all kinds, and don't follow professional sports even a little.

I fit squarely within the stereotypes, and then also not, largely because I was raised by a very strong leader who recognized aspects of himself in me. I was taught to take charge when appropriate and to speak passionately and intelligently. I was taught to expect that men will respect me for my mind and my convictions, not for my ability to stroke someone's fragile ego by playing helpless. I wasn't raised to play dumb, or play cute, or play princess. I learned to work hard, to develop my skills, to contribute on a team and in society, and it drives me bonkers when women depend instead on their sexuality or their fragility. I think there's a better way.

If you're a woman, and you get what you want by batting your eyelashes, faking fragility, or making the most of your push-up bra, and then you wonder why you're not taken seriously in your career or given responsibility in your church, I think you may have believed the reigning cultural lie about what makes us attractive. And if you're a man, and you celebrate femininity only as it presents itself in beauty and tenderness, please consider widening your view of what it means to be a woman. Consider strength, intelligence, passion, and compassion. And certainly, gentlemen, if you still insist on using the word *girly* as a derogatory term, I hate to be the one to say it, but you and the governor of California are both missing the point.

I want businesses and government systems and certainly churches to be led more and more often by women. I believe that men and women would both benefit from it in dozens of ways. But if that's going to happen, I think we have to declare a princess-free zone. No tiaras, no *Girls Gone Wild*, no pretending we can't carry things. No fairytales, no waiting around to be rescued, and absolutely no playing dumb.

Let's set a new example for a generation of young women

who are watching us closely. Let's teach them by our example to be women who work hard, who pay attention to their dreams, who give themselves to making the world a better place, women who believe that there are a whole lot of things more important than being the prettiest princess in the room.

thirty-one

THE HOME TEAM

Lately, I've been working hard on my commitment to the home team. Everybody has a home team: it's the people you call when you get a flat tire or when something terrible happens. It's the people who, near or far, know everything that's wrong with you and love you anyway. The home team people are the ones you can text with five minutes' notice, saying, I'm on my way, and I'm bringing tacos.

There are two reasons you need to know who your home team is. First, you need to know who they are because they need you. These are the people you visit in the hospital no matter what. These are the people whose weddings you attend, no matter how far the destination is or what terrible thing they've chosen for you to wear. These are the ones who tell you their secrets, who get themselves a glass of water without asking when they're at your house. These are the people who cry when you cry. These are your people, your middle-of-the-night, no-matter-what people.

The second reason you need to know who your home team is, is because then you know who your home team is not. Everyone else is everyone else. You may be tempted to have about a hundred close friends and relatives on your home team. I'm not going to tell you exactly how many you can have, but there are a few ways of getting to that number. First, I'll tell you right now that my home team is bigger than average. I'm not bragging. I'm just saying that it takes a village for me to feel really close and connected. My husband, on the other hand, could live perfectly well with about three other people on the whole planet.

And it doesn't last forever, that team. It shifts sometimes, when you move, or as life changes every few years. That's not wrong. But at any given season, you've got to know, essentially, who you're responsible for when it all falls apart.

It's so easy to give everything we have to the first people who ask, or the people who ask the most often, or the people who are always in crisis. But stop yourself: are they a part of your home team?

I'm easily seduced by the idea that I can solve someone's problem. I like solving problems, saving the day, swooping in with the right dress or the right words or the right solution. Because of this, I've been known to offer use of my wedding dress to people I meet on airplanes, to throw parties in honor of people I barely know, and to accept full emotional and psychological responsibility for people I only know from Facebook. These are not my best choices, but I'm working on it.

I'm proud to say that at this point, I don't make coffee

dates with people just because I can't figure out how to say no. This took about ten years and a fair amount of therapy, and I relapse every so often, but for the most part, I try to think about the things only I can do, and only do those. For example, there are a whole lot of people in the world who can have coffee with the perfectly nice lady I met at preschool. She has a home team of her own, and I want to give the best of what I have to mine, because I'm one of the only people who can bring the exact right deli sandwich (#16, no tomatoes) over to Melody's house when she calls to tell me she's having another miscarriage.

There is a totally finite amount of time and energy that each of us have to give to the people in our lives. You can give yours to your home team. Or you can spend it haphazardly on an odd collection of people who need something from you, largely because you don't want to say no and risk what might happen if you do that. This is a terrible reason to be friends with someone, because it's a ticking time bomb of resentment and codependence.

This is the thing: the home team concept for me is not all about getting myself out of the doghouse with a whole bunch of people who need something from me. It's about making sure that the people who deserve my energy and love and attention get it before it's sucked up by people who have their own home teams.

I am one of those people who, as an adult, is actually friends with my parents. Charter members of my home team. They're totally still parents, prone to telling me I look tired and asking how my car's running. But they're also interesting, smart people who make me laugh and make me think. I love to have dinner with them and go on vacation with them and spend Saturday mornings in their garage while Henry helps my dad wash the cars.

My brother, certainly, is part of the home team. During a rough few days earlier this year, he came over just about every other day to sit on my couch and eat chicken fingers with Henry, because that's what the home team does. It shows up when needed. The housechurch, even across the miles, is our home team.

One way you can tell if someone's on your home team is if you'll let them walk right into your house without picking up dirty dishes and checking your hair before they get there. I had a friend with whom I was really trying to build a close, honest relationship, and after almost five years, I still hadn't seen her without her makeup on. If there's makeup on every time you see someone, that doesn't really sound like the home team to me.

This idea of a home team is difficult, I know, and fraught with disaster for people who prefer to believe that they really can meet the needs of the whole universe. What if someone needed something from you, but that person isn't on the home team? There are exceptions, of course. I'm not suggesting that you lock down a list of seven and never help another person again. I'm so thankful for people who've allowed me onto their home teams when I needed it, even though they had a zillion other friends.

The first step is realizing that there is in fact a limited amount of time and caring and energy. I'm generally the last to admit this. I prefer to believe that I am the warrior queen of unlimited relational energy, and that a full calendar is no match for my capacity and skills. Right about then, I get the flu. Or my son does. Or I start crying in the car and can't figure out why. It's usually because I've given more than I should to people who actually aren't a part of my daily, regular world. They're not the ones who need it.

So I'm thinking hard about the home team these days, getting clear on who they are and who they're not, trusting that God in his infinite wisdom can take care of us all, and that show-offy overachievers with savior-complexes need not apply.

thirty-two

AURORA

Welcome to Aurora. After many, many months of paying two mortgages, it's no small answer to our prayers that the house has sold, and it's lovely to already know the family who will be running up and down those stairs, sliding across those floors, riding bikes on that stretch of sidewalk.

You're unpacking, wondering where to put the furniture. We rearranged the living room approximately ninety-seven times over the course of our six years there. It's a tricky one, with so many doors and windows. A few things you might want to know about your new home on Aurora: the living room radiators are the best ones, the showoffs. I used to sit by the window in an overstuffed chair, one hand resting lightly on the radiator for warmth. The drinking fountain in the powder room is a favorite, especially for kids, and the morning light from the east on the three-seasons porch is just the softest, most perfect light, like angel food cake.

I don't know if I believe that you can feel all the things that have happened in a home. Some people can, I think, but most people focus on filling a house with their own brand-new feelings and memories. But if you were to feel, in quiet moments, that the home you are now living in has a good feeling to it, like people have laughed really hard and prayed really honestly and snuggled babies in that home, you'd be right.

We brought Henry home from the hospital to that house, to the pale blue room at the top of the stairs. We had baby showers for Selah, Spence, Emerson, and Mikayla in that house. We walked Henry back and forth over the creaking upstairs floors and around and around the coffee table in the living room. He took his very first steps in the dining room, letting go of the table leg and wobbling toward the chair.

I bet we had a thousand parties in that house—lots of barbecues, usually in the backyard, but once for some reason we brought the grill and the lawn games around to the front and made the party there. I'm sure our neighbors loved that. They'll have all sorts of stories about the tremendously annoying things we did, about drum sets and the time our friends who live in a black school bus stopped over after church and stayed for a very long time.

And maybe sometimes at Aurora you'll sense some ghosts, little shadows of sadness. Maybe you'll sit looking out of the blue room window and think "someone's heart was broken here." You'll be right. Maybe you'll sit in the living room and feel that a desperate and grieving someone had been prayed for, surrounded by friends right on that hardwood floor. You'll be right.

You know, of course, about the Real Food Café. I feel that

many of the seemingly unsolvable issues of marriage, friendship, and writing were indeed solved there over the veggie hash. But you know all this, having lived in practically the same neighborhood all these years. You know about the library's story hour and how that branch of the bank is so preposterously slow.

This is what you might not know: I fought against that house for almost six years. It was too big, too unfamiliar. I wanted desperately to move, particularly back to Chicago, but out of that house, in any case. But staying put in that house all those years taught me something incredibly valuable: when you stay with something instead of walking away, it builds something new inside of you, something solid and weighty, something durable. But you do have to wait for it. You have to earn it the hard way. That house didn't teach me anything the first year. But life and God, over time, used that funny old house to teach me about how nothing is all one thing or all another.

There is, in grown-up life, very little black and white. I tried to cast that house and Grand Rapids as a whole as villains in our fairy tale, but they weren't. That house both drove me crazy and grew me up. I became a mother there, a writer there. I healed from my first big professional failure there and learned to cook there, one of the most life-giving and healing acts I know.

Grand Rapids never did really feel like home, but it taught me some things I want to take with me wherever home is the rest of my life. It was in Grand Rapids that I really learned to feed people around my table. I learned to throw parties in Chicago. Let's be honest, I learned to throw parties in college, but when the only thing on the menu is trash-can punch that you stir with a broom handle, I don't think that counts. In Chicago, I threw cocktail parties and barbecues and Oscar parties, where all I did was open containers I'd bought at the grocery store.

This is the difference: in Chicago you have parties in restaurants and bars and rented rooms, and in Grand Rapids you have them in your home, any home. People open their homes all the time, even if they're not fancy or sprawling, and they feed you largely the food they'd eat even if you weren't there. I love that. In Chicago, only people with really spectacular homes entertain, and if they do, they mostly cater. In Chicago, when you say, *Can I bring something?* you mean wine. But in Grand Rapids, you mean, *Can I bring a homemade soup or a salad with greens from my garden or a warm loaf of bread I've baked myself?*

My friends in Grand Rapids taught me how to have dinner parties, how to accept help with dishes and cleanup, how to make macaroons, and how to invite people into a space that's far from perfect. They taught me that there's a quality in a home that's more important than perfect decorating and that people don't mind folding chairs at all. They taught me that food is best when it's made with love by familiar hands, not delivered in chafing dishes or ordered off a menu. They also taught me how to make a whole lot of things I'd never eaten in Chicago, like a salad that involves both candy bars and marshmallows.

I believe in a very deep way that our past is what brings us to our future. When I pray for someone, I thank God for every day of their life, for every moment, for every heartbreak and each moment of happiness that has brought them to be this person at this time. I believe in mining through the darkest seasons in our lives and choosing to believe that we'll find something important every time.

In my worst moments, I want to slam the door on the hard

parts of our life in Grand Rapids. Deadbolt it, forget it, move forward, happier without it. But I don't want to lose six years of my own history behind a slammed door. So now I'm mining through, searching for light, and the more I look, the more I find. I see the moments of heartbreak that led to honesty about myself I wouldn't have been able to get to any other way.

I see *JulieRuthSara*, three women I always think of in the same breath or thought, just like that: *JulieRuthSara*. When I think of what was actually quite grand in Grand Rapids, those are some of the first faces I see. They taught me and loved me and took me dancing on a whole lot of weeknights. They are three of the most beautiful, expressive, gutsy, passionate women I know.

Sara colored my hair super-bright platinum and chocolate brown and almost every color in between. She gave me her lasagna recipe and also one of the best pieces of advice I've ever received. I was trying to figure out what to do next, worried about what people would think if I did this or that. And she said, "You know, Shauna, people really aren't thinking about you as often as you think they are." Huh. I can't tell you how many times I've repeated that to myself since she said it.

Julie is a singer and a natural childbirth coach and a redhead, as wild and loving and wide open as anyone I've ever known. And Ruth is tall and gorgeous and smart, and when we were both in the roughest of seasons, we drank coffee in her kitchen and cried together about twice a week.

I understand the temptation to draw an angry X through a whole season or a whole town or a whole relationship, to crumple it up and throw it away, to get it as far away as possible from a new life, a new future. But I think that's both the easiest and the most cowardly choice. These days I'm walking over and retrieving those years from the trash, erasing the X, unlocking the door. It's the only way that darkness turns to light. The harder I look, the more I find all sorts of things Grand Rapids gave me. The harder I look, the more thankful I am for what I learned, what I became, what God gave me and what God took away during that season.

Life fell apart for us in that house, several times, like falling down the stairs, when you keep thinking that surely *this* is the bottom, now *this*, now *this*. And God and community and prayer patched us up and tended to our bruises. And now, my friends, it is your house. I hope fewer things break for you than they did for us, both in the house and in your lives. But if things do break, both in the house and in your lives, I pray that they will be repaired with love and wisdom, the same way they were for us. I pray for your children, that this home will keep them warm and safe and happy, and for your marriage, that you will create years of sweet memories under this roof. If you're the sort of people who slow dance in the kitchen, we can tell you from experience that this kitchen is a good one for it.

And on the topic of the kitchen, it is not lost on me that for a long time all I wanted in the world were granite countertops, and because of that little kitchen flood while we were out of town, we got them installed just before we moved out. I sincerely hope you enjoy them. Someone should.

thirty-three

MY PATRON SAINT

My friend Kirsten is two years older than I am, but for whatever reason, when we met she seemed impossibly older, in a good way, like an exotic, world-wise older sister with whom I would never catch up. We met in Europe, students at the same college traveling together for the semester. She's essentially the Technicolor version of me: blonder, louder, curvier, more creative, more fearless, more expressive. She's wilder, brighter, smarter, riskier. She wears the clothes I rip out of magazines while I'm wearing the same gray T-shirt every day for a week. She's me, and then some. She's the me I would be if I could. And even now, separated by a decade, marriages, babies, two thousand miles, she's the older-sister, Tinkerbell voice in my head.

I emailed her at some point while I was supposed to be writing. My friends can always tell when I'm supposed to be writing, because they get lots and lots of emails, like I'm a puppy with a toy who wants to play. I sent her a rambling, complaining email about how hard writing is, and about how I'm no good at it, and about how I'm so not in the right space, mentally. I gave her all sorts of reasons why finishing the book was so not the right thing to do: it was stressing me out and making me cranky and not allowing me to do the things I really felt passionately about, like watching old episodes of *No Reservations* and reading novels and taking naps.

Kirsten is a tender, imaginative soul. She used to have her kitchen painted a very specific sparkly pink to match a pair of feathery angel wings she hung on the wall. She lives in San Francisco, for heaven's sake, land of karma and wine and hippies, so I thought for sure she would cut me a little slack in the name of not feeling it. I thought she'd tell me that it was all right to stop writing, that maybe I should go out and buy myself a pair of fabulous shoes or a cookie.

No such luck. Almost immediately she responded to my email with another email, two pages long, single-spaced. She said things like "Get to work" and "It's not mystical or magical. Just do the writing." She said, "If you let this opportunity pass you by, I will hate you just a little bit forever." She took back the part about hating me at the end of the email, but she did ask me to consider how I'd feel about myself, walking away from this opportunity.

I wanted to be coddled, babied. I wanted someone to buy my excuses and sanction my desire to quit. But she loves me. And she knows me. And in that moment she loved me enough to tell me the truth about myself, about life, and about what matters. Great friendship does a lot of things in our lives, but one of the best things it does is tell us the truth about ourselves when we need it most.

Even though she lives so far away, and it's been so long
since we've lived in the same place, I find myself asking fairly
often what Kirsten would do in a particular situation, because
when I think about things the way she thinks about them,
whatever I'm facing becomes a whole lot clearer. She has a
particular resolve, a sense of self and groundedness that I don't
always have. She's better at making the choices that work for
her, regardless of how common or uncommon they are.

When she and her husband were first married, they lived
in a kooky loft with all sorts of half-levels and windy stairs.
They're both artists and musicians, and their home suited
them perfectly. When she was pregnant with their first son,
they bought a house in Potrero Hill, a big fancy house with a
big heavy mortgage, and she talked about how she felt like a
grown-up—meaning she felt trapped in a job she didn't love
to pay a mortgage for a home she didn't love, all the while
plagued by the nagging feeling that this home was supposed
to make her happy.

Then all at once she and her husband moved to Alameda,
a beachy, lovely island across the bay, leaving the fancy house
in the city still for sale. She said they were moving to save
their lives and their marriage, and that the loss they took on
the house was worth every penny, because it let them breathe
again, let them live again. I've been to their home in Alameda
several times, and for a while the story of Kirsten and her
husband moving there was like a fairy tale or a bedtime
story to me—tell me again! Tell me the one about moving to
Alameda again!

I thought of Kirsten when I finally said out loud, "This
is what I want: I want to live near my family in a little house

with lots of windows." Not rocket science, certainly, but for a girl who sometimes can't make a grocery list because I get so tangled up about what I really want in life, a very big deal.

Catholics have patron saints, individuals who embody something: safe travels or motherhood or lost causes. Kirsten is for me the patron saint of changing your life, of not waiting for someone else to come and rearrange it for you, of not driving a good idea into the ground when it's clear it isn't working, of paying close attention to what you want and need and making it happen.

I have friends who talk to me about, you know, fitness. And I listen politely. They tell me about how fantastic they feel when they run or spin or whatever. I can imagine how that would be, I guess. But they're athletic people, fundamentally. That's the difference. I also have friends who are cat people, and they tell me about how they just love it when Kitty licks their face, or how darling it is to sleep all snuggled up with Mr. Fluffy.

I hate cats. I'm a little bit afraid of them, because they always look at me like they're developing some sort of devious plan, and also because I'm highly allergic to them. I don't ever want Kitty to lick my face, but I understand that people get into that sort of thing. That's how I feel when athletic people talk to me about the glories of working out, like I'm talking to a cat person. I get it, but I'm not going to go out and get a cat.

In the last few years, though, Kirsten has become a runner. A devoted, healthy, strong, long-term, long-distance runner. This is not what I expected. When we first met, she seemed just about like me, and by that I mean, not particularly athletic. When we were in college, we shopped and ate and went dancing together, but we certainly weren't setting the alarm for spin classes or anything.

So when Kirsten became a runner, it threw me for a bit of a loop, in the best possible way. Now this is something to think about. Once again, Kirsten proves to be the patron saint of changing my life. She's like me. And if she can do it, maybe I can do it.

You must know that I have a long and serious aversion to running. My lifetime running experience can be edited down to a compilation video in my mind that scrolls through generally awful memories of feeling self-conscious and close to vomiting, including junior high gym class drills, and a well-intentioned youth pastor who made us get up early at camp and run through the woods, to build character or some such thing.

At one point, somewhere in my twisted adolescent mind, I realized that all the men I admired were married to athletic women, and one of those athletic women coached track at my high school. Determined to transform myself into that kind of woman so that that kind of man would love me, I did one season of high school track. And I was absolutely terrible. I skipped practice and milked minor injuries. I was too slow to sprint and didn't have the endurance for distance, so I ended up being the slowest leg of middle distance relays, and also doing triple jump, which I promise I never did right, even once. Running taps into all my fears about myself, that I'm not strong, that I can't make it, that somewhere between my mind and my body, something important is broken.

Every few years I run one time, out of guilt and self-hatred, and that one time is so terrible that it buys me a few more years of not running. But I'm telling you, this Kirsten thing fascinates me. So I started running, just a tiny bit. Shuffling, really. I don't love it and I'm not great at it, but I do it. And I think about Kirsten when I do it. I think about what she says about it, about how it helps her think and breathe and sleep, about how it brings something to her life that nothing else does. I'm not there yet, clearly. I huff and puff and get blisters and demand that whoever is running with me tells me really funny stories to take my mind off all the jiggling.

But if you're looking for proof that people really can change, look no further. The ultimate non-runner herself is shuffling through the neighborhood, and I'm doing it because of my patron saint. Like so many times in the years we've known each other, Kirsten's showing me what it means to make a life, to craft a way of living and being that works and makes life workable and sweet, and for this time, and every time, I'm thankful.

thirty-four

KNEES OR BUNS

Everything I'm reading these days suggests that good parenting is all about choices. You don't tell your kids what to do, or at least you tell them what to do as rarely as possible, like only when they're going to injure themselves or another person. The rest of the time, you give them choices so that they think they're responsible, functional individuals governing their own destinies. Never mind that Henry is three and governs absolutely nothing. We give him choices, and one of the choices we give him quite often is the choice between knees or buns.

He likes to stand on his chair at the dinner table, at restaurants, anywhere, possibly because it makes him tall and therefore powerful, so he can lord his tallness over the rest of the diners. It's dangerous, not to mention annoying, to be lorded over by a toddler while you're trying to eat. For these reasons, we give him a choice. We look him in the eye, possibly with a hand on his arm, and we tell him that he can make a choice:

knees or buns. He must sit, but he has all the authority in the world to decide if he'd like at this moment to sit on his knees, kneeling, or sit on his buns.

What I'm coming to is that at least for me, writing is a lot like dealing with a toddler. It's helpful for me to feel as though I have choices, and at the very same time, it's helpful for those choices to be extremely narrow, like knees or buns. Henry believes that he is the master of his will, and we're able to enjoy a meal without him jumping off his chair or driving us crazy by patting us on the heads from his newfound position of glory. Everyone wins.

And writing is the same: I need to believe that I have options, but not really have any at all. When I'm writing, I am absolutely free as a bird to sit anywhere in our whole house. At my desk? Certainly. The brown chair by the window? You bet. The couch in the kitchen? It's my world. I can sit anywhere. I'm the master of my fate. I define my destiny.

I, however, cannot get out the tape measure to see what size rug I'd like to order for the living room, and I certainly cannot order it. I cannot wander from room to room collecting assorted members of the Justice League and throwing them back in the toy box. But if I want to move from the guest room bed to the dining room table, again, it's my world.

The same is true for the actual writing. I can write a new essay or edit a rough draft. I can make lists of possible chapters, revise old chapters, work on an overall structure—I have all the freedom in the world. No one tells me what to do. I cannot, however, read the same novel I've been rereading for weeks.

I do find that when I'm writing, I get hungry for lunch at about nine-thirty in the morning. Ravenous and starving as though I've never eaten in my life. I also find that I get very tired, and often I wonder if I'm sick, and if it wouldn't be a good idea to just sleep now and write later. This is when an office with other people would be helpful, because the social pressure would keep me from (a.) eating vast quantities of left-overs standing in front of the fridge and (b.) napping midday. That's why coffee shops are a good idea sometimes, because it's weird to put your head down on the table and just zone out for a while, another thing that's very easy to do at home alone.

I do allow myself to keep a list of things to be done when it's not writing time. I write them down so that I remember to do them sometime, just not now. So far, today's list is: measure for rug, order rug, buy small vacuum, vacuum living room with said vacuum, develop workout plan, execute said workout plan, return Tupperware to Jamie, buy a box of The Good Earth Original tea, buy red shoes for Emily's wedding, and set the DVR to record *Top Chef*.

When I begin to feel trapped and resentful toward all the people who make me write (no one makes me write, of course), I remind myself about all the freedom I really do have: I can sit wherever I want and write about anything I want. I own the world. I have practically unlimited freedom. Of course, all I want to do is eat last night's leftover polenta with meat sauce, cold, standing in front of the fridge, and then go to bed, intermittently rereading a novel between cat naps.

What I learn, over and over, is that writing isn't hard, but sitting down in the chair is really, really hard. So at this point, I'm working at a three-year-old level: knees or buns? I can sit anywhere I like, but I have to sit down, and then the hardest part is over.

Lots of days I feel like I can't grab on to anything concrete, like writing is imaginary and difficult, a mental universe I can't locate. I could cook, unpack, fix, fold, anything tactile and touchable. I'd rather do sit-ups for an hour than try to locate a string of words in my mind. I want to believe that our brains are machines you turn on and off like cars, but when it comes down to it, I think they're a lot more like cats or toddlers: you sometimes have to trick them or turn your back just for a second, allowing them to believe you're not watching.

I can tell you with some authority what certainly, absolutely doesn't help: googling yourself, or checking your blog comments every six minutes, or gluing your eyeballs to Facebook when you're feeling crumbly. I think going online and reading about yourself when you're feeling sad is a recipe for depression. It's like having cold pizza in your fridge, how you can practically hear it audibly calling out for you to eat it. You know you'll feel terrible after you eat six slices in the middle of the night with the refrigerator door still open, but you want to and then when you do, you feel terrible, partially because that much cold pizza in the middle of the night would make anyone sick, and partially because you knew better, because this has happened a thousand times before, and you feel silly and weak, like the pizza ate you and not the other way around.

I speak from experience, both with the pizza-eating and the reading about oneself online, and neither ever makes you feel anything but awful. Even if, say, nine out of ten reviews on Amazon are lovely, that one less-than-glowing review will dive into your psyche like a virus you absolutely can't shake.

Generally, when you're stuck, don't read about other people online either. If you're feeling scared and small, your twisted-up mind will make them into heroes and paragons of talent and virtue. All you'll notice are the fun things they're doing that you're not and how skinny they are in their pictures. All the status updates and tweets, when you're feeling jittery and terrified, somehow line up one after another in this vein: "Just got back from 45 days in Hawaii." "My new army of housekeepers is cleaning my house top to bottom." "Sifting through awards and invitations from journalists and reviewers who think I'm a genius." It's not really like that, of course. Mostly people are talking about how badly they need a coffee and what they thought about the new *Vampire Weekend* album and how frustrated they are that their kids won't nap. But when you're stuck, all you see are the ones that make you feel tiny and gray, like dryer lint.

Another reason to close your browser when you're feeling stuck creatively is that your stuckness makes you vulnerable to the myth of the makeover, that if you just do or buy a few new things, you might stop being your same terrible self all the way around. By the way, this vein of reasoning is responsible for every bad hair decision I've ever made. Last year I was trying to solve the big question of who I am in the universe, and in a tender, split-open moment, I thought, *Maybe as a brunette, I'll feel at home in this unforgiving world.*

You know how that story ends, of course. Months of looking like I had chronic fatigue, punctuated by emergency visits to get the blonde back and a covenant with my stylist and very good friend Sara that I never do such a terrible thing again. It's a good thing I don't have access to bleach and scissors in my writing room or I'd be a whole new awful me twice a week.

Creativity isn't easy, and it isn't something you turn on like a light switch. My inbox will tell you that the world is full of writers who don't write, painters who don't paint, dancers who don't dance. They want me to tell them something, ostensibly a secret something that will get them up and moving again, creating again. My reply is always a disappointing one: I don't know what to tell you. Sit down, knees or buns. But then I tell them something else, too: do it for the feeling you'll have when you're done. Making art doesn't have the instant payoff that most things in our modern lives do, but like all things that really matter, the big payoff is invisible and comes much later.

Yesterday my friend Meredith came over and we made meat sauce together. We talked and diced and stirred and tasted and made adjustments, and then let the sauce simmer for a long time. And you could taste the time it took, the layers of flavor—red wine, rosemary, garlic, a couple different kinds of tomatoes. That's how it is when you give yourself to something: it takes time and love and stirring, but at the end, no one would mistake it for quick sauce.

thirty-five

EVERGREEN

I t's the first real snowfall of the year, fine flakes falling
steadily. They're falling fast and straight down, not a hint
of wind. It always feels like things are quieter when it's snow-
ing, like the falling of the flakes absorbs the noise, blanketing
everything with a hush. I keep remembering little things from
last December—moments from the work trip that took me to
Northern California: the Candy Cane Joe-Joe's Monica and I
ate on the bed at our hotel in Folsom, the bed-and-breakfast
Kirsten and I stayed at in Palo Alto, and the huge slab of lasagna we shared at the Italian restaurant we walked to for dinner
one night. I remember the dresses I wore to all the Christmas
events, with black tights and high patent leather Mary Janes.
I remember the smell of gingerbread coffee and the enchiladas
we had on New Year's Eve, our housechurch together for the
first time in a year.

I remember that last December I wanted to skip through

210

Christmas, that I didn't even want to go to the parties. All I wanted was a new year. We knew we'd be moving at the end of January, but December just dragged on and on. All I wanted was to get to January, get to the move, get to a future I'd been longing for.

This December feels so different. All of life feels so different. I saw an old friend last week, and as we caught up, she told me about her job, a temporary one, and her living situation, a temporary one. She lost her job earlier this year, and that loss hasn't yet worked its way out of her life. She's one of the most joyful, exuberant people I know, but as we talked, I could tell she was exhausted and scared, and that this season has been a heartbreaking one.

Oh, I get it, I told her. I get where you are right now. I know what it's like to long for a new year, I know what it's like to feel like everything's on hold and you don't recognize your own life even though it's right in front of you. I know what it's like when the things that always used to make you happy don't do the trick anymore, because they can't break through the sadness and fear that are covering over everything in your life.

I was there, I said, and I'm not there anymore, and I'm so thankful. You'll get through this, and you'll find yourself in an entirely new place. You'll find your old self again. You'll laugh easily and sleep well. It will happen. *I promise.*

Last December, even the sweetest things were weighed down by fear and anxiety and exhaustion. I remember New Year's Eve with the housechurch at the cabin. We laughed and ate guacamole and drank beer margaritas, and in the morning when we burned the bacon while we were making breakfast together, I almost burst into tears, overwhelmed by something that totally didn't matter. With friends one night, I got my feelings terribly hurt, not because anyone was cruel, but because those days I was so tender and raw that practically everything hurt.

I was afraid, then, that it would always be like that. I was afraid that this was the new normal, that seasons of lightness and peace were over in my life, and this brittle, fractured way of living would last forever.

And then we moved. When I'm being careless, I chalk it all up to the move. But it wasn't just that. It was a thousand things that had gotten broken along the way as I plodded through a very bleak season, and then a thousand opportunities to put them back together. It was prayer, friendship, rest, writing, patience, discipline. It was gifts I didn't and don't deserve, and also hard choices I made, ones that made me proud of myself for the first time in a long time. I went to a couple different doctors and a therapist. I started writing again and started sleeping well again. I began to pray with more hope and possibility, and little by little, some of the stuck things became unstuck.

Everyday life became a little easier once again, and little things didn't make me cry nearly as often. I stopped eating colossal amounts of the foods that make me feel terrible, and for the first time in a long time I made it a habit to send myself to bed when I was tired. Life stopped feeling so frantic and lonely. I wasn't traveling all the time. I was surrounded by old friends and family, and that made me feel safe for the first time in years. I went to church every Sunday and began to volunteer there, and I felt nourished by the ideas and practices, at home in a very important way. It wasn't all one thing, but a thousand big and little things, and for every single one of them, I'm thankful.

When things are dark and splintering, I get stuck, believing that it will always be how it is right now, that new life will never come, that change will never really break into my life. But this year is all the proof I need. One year ago today, a similarly snowy, lush day, it was all different, and I want to hold this moment like a charm—*remember, remember.* The snow is falling on the evergreen tree in our new backyard, and our cozy little house feels warm and safe. I'm wrapped in a blanket that's been dragged to every home we've lived in since we got married—new couch, new view, same old yellow blanket. A candle flickers on the table, and the steam from my tea smells like cloves. We are a million miles from last December, and I want to keep this moment with me as a reminder of what can happen in a year.

Anything can happen in a year. Broken down, shattered things can be repaired in a year. Hope can grow in a year, after a few seasons of lying dormant. I didn't like who I was or how I was living a year ago, but I didn't know any other way to do it. I recognize the face that stares back at me in the mirror these days. When I look into my own eyes, I recognize a person I thought was lost, and I feel whole, for the first time in years.

I don't know where you are these days, what's broken down and what's beautiful in your life this season. I don't know if this is a season of sweetness or one of sadness. But I'm learning that neither last forever. There will, I'm sure, be something that invades this current loveliness. That's how life is. It won't be sweet forever. But it won't be bitter forever either. If everywhere you look these days, it's wintery, desolate, lonely, practice believing in springtime. It always, always comes, even though on days like today it's nearly impossible to imagine, ground frozen, trees bare and spiky. New life will spring from this same ground. This season will end, and something entirely new will follow it.

As I look out the window, the snowflakes are bigger now and falling even faster. People are wondering about canceling events for tonight and school closings for tomorrow. That would be just fine with me. I have all I need right here: this evergreen, this tea, this candle, this December.

thirty-six

THE MIDDLE

Two years ago, at the end of a green and windy June, we had one of those nights that I'm still thinking about. I don't totally know why. I just know that sometimes it all comes together, in us and between us and around us, and even years later, the quality of that evening or that moment impresses itself upon our hearts, like wearing a locket under your shirt, your own secret memory all day long, bouncing against your skin.

I remember days and places by remembering meals and smells and tastes, especially meals I've cooked, not because they've been the best meals, by any means, but because they've been the ones that my hands and my senses remember, cilantro coming to life as I slice through it, avocados and jalapeños and lime becoming more than the sum of their parts under the back of a spoon.

It was a scheduling nightmare, actually, one of those plans that any sane person would have abandoned. But one of the most cracked-up and crazy parts of me is the part that absolutely will not allow me to call off party plans. If the world ends all around us one day, it's entirely possible that while the sky falls, I'll be handing out drinks and taking coats, squeezing in just one more party. On this particular Sunday night at the lake, our dinner guests were tired, coming bedraggled and late from all corners. Also, most of them had never met. No matter, I said, and soldiered on.

Aaron had been in Canada for the week and arrived just as the other guests were arriving. My editor Angela and her husband, David, were in town for a wedding, and I asked them to come to the lake for dinner. My dear friend Sara had just played wedding planner/problem solver/miracle worker for her sister's wedding up north, and I invited her to come down and see us on her way back to Boston. Sunday dinners in South Haven are their own tradition, so a usual cast of South Haven friends joined us, too.

Everyone arrived right at the same time, it seemed, texts and directions and last-minute calls interrupting us in the kitchen, and then all of a sudden the house was full. I had pulled out a stack of recipes I'd been wanting to try: pork chops with fresh cherry sauce, grilled chicken with apricot ginger glaze. As is our tradition, I put people right to work. I met Angela's husband David for the first time and then handed him a knife and a pound of cherries from the farmer's market. James opened the wine, and Sara and Angela set the table. Jodi brought her bok choy salad, the one with dried cranberries and almonds, the one I always request. Everyone else grilled and played bocce ball and watched Henry run around the yard, and as the sun set, we gathered at the table, shoulder to shoulder, friends and strangers.

We were tired from our various weeks, staring at unfamiliar faces, trying to remember names and make conversation
as we passed the food around the table. And then, just like it
always does, after a little while food and wine and time around
the table braided us together, and we started telling stories
and jokes, connecting to what the last person said, laughter
bubbling through.

We talked about work, which is usually the boring-est
conversation ever for a dinner party. But around our table that
night we had Angela, my editor, letting us in on the business
with a dry smile. We had James, an environmental policy graduate student at Harvard, and David, an aeronautical engineer.
My mother's latest areas of interest are the Middle East peace
process and nuclear nonproliferation, and Sara finished her
dissertation on James Joyce just in time to work on the Obama
campaign. Clearly we were not at a loss for interesting topics.
We laughed and told stories and asked questions and pro-
nounced the cherry sauce on the pork chops a keeper. While
the men cleared the table and did dishes together, the women
went out to the porch and watched the moon on the water,
possibly the best of all of our South Haven traditions. And
when it was very late, we hugged goodbye, sending people off
down the long driveway, yelling directions and thanks.

And then life, of course, rolled on after that. Sara went
back to Boston, Angela and David back to Charleston. What I
didn't know at the time was that there was already a problem
with my pregnancy, and that two days later we'd learn of the
miscarriage and complications.

That night stayed with me, possibly more than any other
night that summer, even though there were plenty of lovely

nights. As I thought about it, I realized that night was right absolutely in the middle of the hardest season Aaron and I had yet experienced, a long stretch of uncertainty and fear. And maybe that's why that night stands out. Because it was an oasis, a port in the storm, a moment of levity and connection in the middle of a season that felt distinctly lonely and tangled. In a season of darkness, it was a burning flame, warm and healing. And maybe that's one of the greater gifts. When you're in the middle, pretty much all you can ask for are little bits of flame to light the darkness that feels interminable.

You don't know what the story is about when you're in the middle of it. You think you do, but you don't. You make up all kinds of possible story lines: This is about growing up. Or this is about living without fear. You can guess all you want, but you don't know. All you can do is keep walking.

There is nothing worse than the middle. At the beginning, you have a little arrogance, loads of buoyancy. The journey, whatever it is, looks beautiful and bright, and you are filled with resolve and silver strength, sure that whatever the future holds, you will face it with optimism and chutzpah. It's like the first day of school, and you're wearing the outfit you laid out last night, backpack full of perfectly sharpened yellow pencils.

And the end is beautiful. You are wiser, better, deeper. You know things you didn't previously know, you've shed things you previously clung to. The end is revelation, resolution, a soft place to land.

But, oh, the middle. I hate the middle. The middle is the fog, the exhaustion, the loneliness, the daily battle against despair, and the nagging fear that tomorrow will be just like today, only you'll be wearier and less able to defend yourself against it. The middle is the lonely place, when you can't find words to say how deeply empty you feel, when you try to connect but you feel like thick glass is separating you from the rest of the world, isolating and deadening everything.

Looking back on the middle, what helped me make it through were nights like that one, with the bok choy salad and the laughter. I don't know if there's anything that can make time pass more quickly when you're in that place, and I don't know if anything good comes from trying to explain again how lost you feel. But what got me through the middle were moments like that Sunday night dinner. There were others, too: dinner on Sara's back porch with Ruth and Julie, the lights strung up to look like an Italian street fair. Pasta and artichokes in white wine at Sarah's house, new faces and old ones around her table on a cold winter evening. A thousand nights at Annette's before she moved, with all the usual suspects— Julie, Ruth, both Sara and Sarah, and all the staples—Irish cheese, dark chocolate, dried fruit, and sparkling wine.

I'm beginning to think that's all you can ask for, in those seasons, for sweet moments of reprieve in the company of people you love. You'll still wake up in the night with the same old fears, and you'll still face the same tired eyes in the morning, but for a few hours, you'll feel protected from it all by the goodness of friendship and life around the table, and for a few hours, that's the best thing I can imagine.

thirty-seven

STEAK FRITES

Last night for our anniversary Aaron and I went to Marché, a French restaurant that we used to go to years ago but hadn't visited in ages, where they serve the best steak frites I've ever had, with perfect little cups of béarnaise and red wine sauce. The restaurant is part *Moulin Rouge* and part *Alice in Wonderland*, deep reds and blues and golds, with umbrellas hanging from the ceiling and super-oversized drum lampshades.

For the first couple years, it seemed like anniversaries were a little like birthdays when you're in your midtwenties—seriously, it's an accomplishment to just stay alive another year? We get to go out for a fancy dinner just because we stayed married? I like a fancy dinner as much as the next girl, but it seemed like a lot of fuss for just making it through.

That's what I used to think, before several good friends' marriages ended, before I experienced firsthand just how difficult marriage can be, before we faced our hardest season yet by far. I wouldn't say we have a hard marriage, but I'd say we had a really hard season. This year, we understand that staying married is indeed an accomplishment, and that staying married well—connected and intimate and giving—sometimes requires every last thing we have to give.

If you've been married long enough, and if life has been hard enough, if you're very honest, you've had tiny, nearly invisible moments when you look over at that person, watching TV or getting a glass of water and you think, *Who is this person? How did we get here?*

You never feel this on your wedding day. You can't even imagine it on your wedding day. But life invades, and brokenness and immaturity and sin invade and all of a sudden, there you are, and you start to believe that you might not ever be able to get back to where you were, all shiny and perfect and bursting with love, on your wedding day.

What does it mean that neither of us can remember what we did for last year's anniversary? I even checked the calendar on my computer—the day is blank. I think maybe we went to Rose's or The Green Well, but it certainly didn't impress itself deeply on our minds. We could tell ourselves it was because we were just moving back from the lake, a month after the miscarriage. We could blame it on the fact that the week of our anniversary, we had our kitchen torn apart, had the world's largest garage sale, and still didn't know if we were moving to Chicago or not.

But you don't forget anniversary dinners because things are busy. You forget anniversary dinners because you both know that you didn't have much to celebrate that year. And thankfully, blessedly, this anniversary feels really different than the last. We're *back* this year, back to the connected, rich way of living we'd experienced up until the last season, and we're glad to be back. We've weathered something, and it's added a layer of sweetness and appreciation and depth to our life together.

For a while we were alternately at each other's throats or isolated under the same roof. We said terrible things to one another, gripped tightly to unrealistic expectations, failed to forgive, even when we promised we would. But we're inching our way back, and I'm so grateful. We're back because we began listening to each other at what seemed like the last possible moment. We were heading for a crash and we both knew it, and turned to one another in the nick of time—*Okay, tell me again. Really, tell me.*

In our best, gutsiest, most honest moments of the last year, we said things to each other that we never imagined saying out loud to anyone, things we were afraid of, things we couldn't bear. And those ugly honest confessions bloomed into a new intimacy, a new protectiveness, a new promise to walk together, and better than before. The connectedness of marriage is almost like being a twin, knowing someone's voice and hands and language as well as you know your own, and the honesty of it, right at the core, when you get to the core, is stunning.

Marriage is more than a contract, with partners and stipulations and *if you, then I* arrangements. It's a messy, beautiful, living, breathing thing, full of dreams and history and patterns and memories, and this is the deal: you can make your point all day long, and you can even be right about your point, but if you stop listening, if you stop really hearing and seeing that other person, something fundamental will be lost. You can try to push and pull all you want, hoping for change. But more often than not, if you do that, I think you'll find two people bruised and exhausted, but not really changed.

So on our eighth anniversary, we're shoring up the distance we created and working hard to recapture the good things that have been there all along. We're working on loving each other just as we are right now: unfinished, unvarnished, in the middle of all the mess, in some ways really different from one another, and in some ways very similar. This year we've decided to lay off each other, to trust that life and God and pain will instruct us when necessary. We're committed to helping each other through those moments, instead of pouring salt in raw wounds and pushing on tender spots, our immaturity disguised as altruistic desire for the other to grow. In some moments during the last season, we wanted the other to grow because it would have suited our needs better, and that's not nearly good enough a reason. We tried to teach one another lessons that we realized after the fact weren't ours to teach. Life will teach us things, and there are times for marriage to teach us, but there are also times for marriage to be a safe landing spot when life is instructing us rather brutally.

In the space that's been created now that we've let a few things go, we're finding all sorts of beautiful things blooming into life once again—the reasons we fell in love, the things we used to laugh about that stopped being funny for a while and are now, blessedly, funny again.

The specifics of that season, we're finding, are not nearly as important as the things that have stayed the same: Aaron is still the most fascinating person I've ever met, the most creative, most truly original person I've ever known. And I can still make him laugh really hard, no small thing. We love to be together as much now as we did back then, feet touching as we read in bed or at a concert of a band he loves or a restaurant I've been dying to try. What brought us together still holds us together, and what we've learned in this last season helps to bind that original connection even more tightly.

I was not afraid during that dark season that Aaron and I were going to split up. I didn't think either of us were going to cheat or leave. But I was, in my most private, fearful moments, afraid that the damage would be irreparable, and that we would slide into being one of those couples who has closed their hearts to one another in the deepest way. We'd continue to live together and raise a child together and watch TV together at night after long days. But I was afraid we'd lose that thing, that deep trust and connection, that willingness to be vulnerable and to try again and risk being hurt again. That's what I was afraid of.

And of all the things I'm thankful for right now, the restored connection between us might be at the top of the list. We made it through and into a new, better place. And so maybe that's what I want to tell you, if you're married and you think the damage is done. I thought that, too, a couple times over the last few years. But our hearts are more elastic than we think, and the work of forgiveness and transformation and growth can do things you can't even imagine from where you're standing now.

When we first got married, we used to say to each other, this is the love story of my life. *You're the love story of my life.* And it's as true as ever tonight. It's a good love story, one about redemption and growth and forgiveness and repairing the damage two people can incur if they're not careful.

People joke about the seven-year itch, and they ask, with various euphemisms, how you keep the spark alive after the honeymoon is over. I'm sure there are as many answers to that question as there are married couples, but I'll tell you something that we've found. You know what's really, really sexy eight years into a marriage? Apologies. Nothing has connected and reconnected us more than honesty, than taking responsibility, than seeing the damage we've wrought and working hard to make it right. Around our house, apologies are sexy.

The best gifts we can give each other this year are apologies and acceptance, gifts we should have been giving one another all along, but forgot for a season, in the midst of hurt feelings and tangled conversations. So here we are: saying we're sorry, letting go, accepting, listening closely for the first time in a long time.

Happy anniversary, Aaron. I know we'll remember this one, and not just for the steak frites.

thirty-eight

BLUEBERRIES

My Grandma Hybels passed away on Sunday night with one of her daughters at her side. Earlier that day, she'd been surrounded by all five of her children and her pastor, and they prayed together, kissed her, held her hands. She was not afraid, and she was not alone.

At her eighty-fifth birthday party this summer, it was apparent to all of us that the cancer had returned and that it was overtaking her body, even though she didn't want to admit it to anyone. As the fall progressed, so did the cancer, and just after Christmas, she was moved to a hospice center. Her last weeks were filled with visits from her children, grandchildren, and great-grandchildren, until late one night, she passed away gently in her sleep.

When, in the weeks before her death, the cousins shared some of our childhood memories with Grandma, there were three things that came up over and over: blueberries, cinnamon toast, and beach glass. Grandma made the very best blueberry pie, and when my cousin Cameron learned that Grandma recently passed her recipe on to his little sister Melody, he told Mel that he expected Grandma's blueberry pie every time he comes to Chicago. We all remember picking blueberries with Grandma at DeGrandchamp's in South Haven, which, for out-of-towners, is widely known as the Blueberry Capital of the World, complete with a Blueberry Festival, Blueberry Parade, and Blueberry Queen.

At Grandma's cottage we ate blueberries straight out of the bowl in the mornings, and in muffins all day long, but our favorite was her fresh blueberry pie, with a scoop of Sherman's Ice Cream—the second most famous export to come out of South Haven, right behind the blueberries.

In the last days of Grandma's life, she had no appetite, and everyone who visited her worked hard to find something that sounded good to her—macaroni or pudding, something. At a certain point, nothing worked. And then my Aunt Marilyn found one last bag of frozen blueberries in Grandma's freezer and brought it to the hospice center. Grandma said that she'd been saving that bag for her great-grandchildren, but admitted that they did sound good, and she'd just have a few. For the last few days of her life, those frozen blueberries were the only things she ate, and for anyone who knew her, that doesn't surprise us a bit.

My brother remembers sitting on the carpet watching *Dukes of Hazzard* at the cottage, because the rule was that if you had already been swimming, you had to sit on the green shag carpet—no wet buns on the couch. When we were done at the beach for the day, Grandma would line us all up in the front yard and spray us all off in one fell swoop, first all our fronts and then all our backs. She was forever fighting against sand in the cottage, but with so many little feet, I think the sand generally won.

We fought over who would get to sleep in Grandma's bed with her, the big brass bed, and in the mornings, we all loved having cinnamon bread from Bunde's Bakery in the sunroom, the toaster and the butter dish in the corner always ready for us.

One of our favorite things to do at Grandma's cottage was to search for beach glass, because Grandma collected it in jars like a precious treasure. Every few days we'd take out all the pieces and spread them out on the dining room table with her, and she acted as though we'd found gold every time.

When we came to visit Grandma for the last time, she gave each of us a box, one for each child and grandchild. In each of our boxes, she had packed up every baby picture, every card we'd given her, and an assortment of family memories and newspaper clippings. Late one night I spread the contents of the box all over my dining room table—baby pictures of my dad that look just like Henry, an invitation to my parents' wedding, and another to my grandparents' wedding. I found a note that my dad wrote to his dad, who passed away when I was two. The contents of that box helped piece together childhood memories long forgotten and bits of a past I never knew.

One thing that brought her great joy in the last several years of her life was time with her great-grandchildren. Grandma held them and soothed them, played with them on the floor, and collected pictures of them to show her friends and sisters. It was a very moving thing to watch Grandma care for our children in much the same ways she cared for us when we were small.

Luka was born less than two months ago, and my cousin Larissa and her husband, Matt, knew, in the first terrifying hours of Luka's life, when he was hooked up to monitors and things seemed to change from moment to moment, that Grandma was praying consistently for Luka's health. And even though she was very sick, she insisted on visiting Luka, and wanted to hold him every chance she got, even when he was fussing.

Just last week, after Grandma had moved to the hospice center, her health declining by the day, she was delighted to hear that my cousin Jake's wife, Sara, gave birth to a son named Logan. While Grandma never wanted to bother anyone about anything, that morning, she wanted to make phone calls to tell people about the birth of baby Logan. In many ways, that's all you need to know about my grandma, that days before the end of her life, her greatest concern was not for herself but for a child, and for the health and safety of her family.

Above all else, even above the blueberries and the cinnamon bread, what we remember about Grandma, what we knew was most important to her, was her faith. She prayed for us consistently and asked us pointedly about where we were going to church and what we were learning from our Bible reading. She modeled for us, more than anything, her deep belief that faith is the center of everything, the foundation upon which all else is built.

At the heart of Grandma's faith was servanthood. She didn't want to be the center of attention and didn't ask hardly anything of anyone. Even at the very end of her life, when she needed something from the nurses, she'd ask, "Would that be too much trouble for you?" They teased her and finally started telling her, "Jerry, this is about you!" Anyone who knew her knows that she never, ever thought it was about her.

On the last afternoon Todd and I spent with her, we talked about the importance of faith. She told us that all she wanted at the end of her life was to know that each one of her children and grandchildren trusted Christ with their lives. I don't think she cared a bit if we went to good colleges or not, or how we looked, or if we made a lot of money. She cared about our spiritual well-being and prayed fervently and consistently for each one of us.

If you opened Grandma's refrigerator, it looked like all she ate was yogurt, cottage cheese, and sour cream. But if you took a closer look you realized that there were odds and ends of all sorts of things in those reused containers—bits of casserole, leftovers, slices of pie all stored in rinsed-out yogurt and cottage cheese containers. She also took crackers and sugar packets from restaurants, and used bread bags to store almost anything. Grandma never wasted a thing and was never extravagant. She didn't spend on herself and lived with great frugality, preferring to give to her church, to missions, and to her family.

Although she lived simply, she gave generously to us. And possibly even more important, she modeled to us her deeply held belief that money doesn't buy happiness, that it isn't ours in the first place, and that wastefulness and extravagance lead to bad ends. In a world where financial mismanagement and recklessness seem to be the norm, we consider it a gift to have learned another way from Grandma.

In my last conversation with Grandma, we talked a lot about heaven. She told me she was so excited to go there and that she felt like it was taking a long time. One of the reasons she was most excited about heaven is because there she'll be reunited with her husband. For a woman who had been widowed for more than thirty years, I can't imagine the sweetness of that reunion. She spoke in great detail about wanting to see her sisters and brothers and looking forward to a time when age and disease and pain are gone.

We'll miss Grandma terribly. We'll think of her every time we eat blueberries or find a piece of beach glass in South Haven. But we know, with as much certainty as we know anything, that she is in heaven, free from pain and disease, reunited with Christ, with a husband she's missed for three decades, and with the brothers and sisters she loved dearly. And for that, we're so thankful.

The best way to honor my grandma's life, I believe, is to live with the faith, simplicity, prayerfulness, and kindness that she lived with every day. When any of us—her children, her grandchildren, the many people she touched and walked with—live simply in order to give generously, when we serve without wanting recognition, when we put the needs of others above our own, when we pray for the people we love, we will honor the legacy of this tiny, lovely, godly woman, my grandma, Gertrude Hybels.

thirty-nine

PHOENIX

When I look back at this most recent season, what I see are a thousand things I wish I would have done differently. I wish I would have been more patient. I wish I would have depended more heavily on the words of Scripture and the biblical pattern of life after death. I wish I wouldn't have eaten so much pizza, especially late at night.

What kept me stuck, when I was stuck, were my own demands and expectations, my own collection of fear and anxiety. And what got me through, when I got through, were the times I spent with people I loved and the times I spent in prayer. It's pretty much that clear, looking back on it all now.

I'm more certain than ever that prayer is at the heart of transformation. And also that God's will has a lot more to do with inviting us to become more than we previously have been than about getting us to one very specific destination. God's will, should we choose to engage in it, will generally feel like surgery, rooting out all the darkness and fear we've come to live with.

My friend Steve says that God doesn't speak to everyone the same way, but that he generally speaks the same way over and over again to each person. I think that's absolutely true. God generally speaks to me through grand gestures. Actually I think he speaks to me first in whispers, and that I don't listen until he's shouting. I regret this, and I think the last few years could have been a little easier had I been a better listener.

But I'm learning. It's human to struggle. It's human to nurse a broken heart, to wonder if the pain will ever let up, to howl through your tears every once in a while. And the best, most redeeming, exciting thing I can imagine, from the smashed-up, broken place I've been, is that something beautiful could blossom out of the wreckage. That's the goal.

And when we're deep in the wreckage, I have to remind myself from time to time that it's okay to cry. My friend Eve told me once that the ability to cry is a sign of health, because it means your body and your soul agree on something, and that what your soul is feeling, your body is responding to. I tell my husband that every time my own personal waterworks turn on. Sign of health, honey.

In the same way that tears are a gift and a sign of health, what I'm coming to learn is that pain is, among other things, an opportunity to learn something about our bodies, a chance to listen to them and learn what they have to teach us. And pain is an opportunity to be comforted, something I always resist, greatly preferring immediate solutions or independence.

My friend Mindy pushed and worked and overworked and kept running past all the signs she should have paid attention to, until one morning she found she had vertigo so bad she couldn't get out of bed. Our bodies know what they're doing, and they know how to get our attention. It's like a toddler asking the same question over and over and over until you think you might lose your mind.

I don't know why some people live with chronic pain and some people don't. I don't have any idea why some bodies are strong and able and others seem to fail at every turn. I have a young friend who was recently diagnosed with diabetes, after she was rushed to the hospital just before a full diabetic coma. Another dear friend lives with epilepsy and another with debilitating Lyme disease. They are young and beautiful, and I don't have any idea why disease has come to live in their bodies and not somewhere else.

But I know that just like emotional pain, physical pain is an opportunity. And it's one that I squander almost every time. When I'm in pain, I whimper and whine and snap at my husband. I use it as an excuse to be a little short with Henry and have an extra glass of wine.

I used to think that the growth we experience through pain, physical or not, was a consolation prize. I used to think it was like having a good personality. Who wants a good personality when you can have legs for days or a face that launches a thousand ships? I thought that what we really want are easy lives, and if we can't have those, then we can at least become deep, grounded people who grow through heartbreak.

But I don't know anyone who has an easy life forever. Everyone I know gets their heart broken sometime, by something. The question is not, will my life be easy or will my heart break? But rather, when my heart breaks, will I choose to grow?

Sometimes in the moments of the most searing pain, we think we don't have a choice. But we do. It's in those moments that we make the most important choice: grow or give up. It's easy to want to give up under the weight of what we're carrying. It seems sometimes like the only possible choice. But there's always, always, always another choice, and transformation is waiting for us just beyond that choice.

This is what I know: God can make something beautiful out of anything, out of darkness and trash and broken bones. He can shine light into even the blackest night, and he leaves glimpses of hope all around us. An oyster, a sliver of moon, one new bud on a black branch, a perfect tender shoot of asparagus, fighting up through the dirt for the spring sun. New life and new beauty are all around us, waiting to be discovered, waiting to be seen.

I'm coming to think there are at least two kinds of pain. There's the anxiety and fear I felt when we couldn't sell our house. And then there's the sadness I felt when I lost the baby or when my grandma passed away. Very different kinds of pain. The first kind, I think, is the kind that invites us to grow. The second kind is the kind that invites us to mourn.

God's not trying to teach me a lesson through my grandma's death. I wasn't supposed to love her less so the loss hurt less acutely. I'm not supposed to feel less strongly about the horror of death and dying. When we lose someone we love, when a dear friend moves away, when illness invades, it's right to mourn. It's right to feel deep, wrenching sadness.

But then there's the other kind of pain, that first kind. My friend Brian says that the heart of all human conflict is the phrase "I'm not getting what I want." When you're totally honest about the pain, what's at the center? Could it be that you're not getting what you want? You're getting an invitation to grow, I think, as unwelcome as it may be.

It's sloppy theology to think that all suffering is good for us, or that it's a result of sin. All suffering can be used for good, over time, after mourning and healing, by God's graciousness. But sometimes it's just plain loss, not because you needed to grow, not because life or God or anything is teaching you any kind of lesson. The trick is knowing the difference between the two.

In my first job out of college, one of the people I worked with just drove me crazy. He pushed my buttons and hurt my feelings and twisted my words, and I couldn't get past it. After months and months, my genius boss Greg told me a couple things: First, he said, "You're not crazy. You're not making this stuff up. He's a difficult person to work with." I exhaled, vindicated, feeling like a deeply discerning person. But then Greg said something else: "You're not wrong about this guy, but why does it bother you so much? Why does his way of being make you so crazy?"

Then he added: "It's okay if you don't know now. The good thing is that you'll have plenty of chances to figure it out, because when someone or something taps into your deep emotion like that, God will keep sending that same kind of person or same kind of situation into your life over and over until you choose to do the work of understanding it and growing past it."

That was over ten years ago, and Aaron and I still talk about that conversation and those words all the time, because we're finding that it's absolutely true. You can learn it the first time, or you'll find that same situation or same kind of person or same opportunity staring you in the face over and over again. You'll wonder at the coincidence for a while. What are the chances that I have to keep working with people like this? What are the chances that my husband and I keep having the same fight over and over? What are the chances that so many different people would hurt my feelings in just the same way?

And there it is, an opportunity to grow, to transcend and transform, to break that terrible pattern. I'm beginning slowly to recognize my own fears and landmines—why some changes are so scary for me, how the crazy-meter ratchets up little by little. I notice these things now and pay attention. And when we pay attention and when we grow, we become freer, more flexible, more faithful, more able to ask for help. We become less fearful, more able, more comfortable with the idea of life as a beautiful mess.

You want me to say that when you grow, finally, all the changes will stop, but they don't. There will be another one, another opportunity to grow, to shed your skin, to rise like a phoenix from the ashes, to break out of your cocoon like a perfect new butterfly.

The clichés and the references to mythology and classic literature abound, because that's what we're all trying to do: we're all trying to emerge new from the pain, beautiful after the brokenness, to live, in fact, that central image of Christianity—life after death.

forty

YOUR STORY
MUST BE TOLD

When my friend Doug told me that the pattern of death and rebirth is the central metaphor of the Christian life, he was giving me the currency that he earned through his own brokenness. He was telling me something that God had written on his life as a part of his story. The reason I didn't understand it at that point was because I didn't need to, but then several years later, I did.

You tell what you know, what you've earned, what you've learned the hard way. You watch it fall on what seem to be deaf ears, and you mutter something under your breath, something about pearls before swine. But then ten years later you realize that one fragment of your story has now been woven into someone else's, a very necessary thing, a bridge to a new way of understanding and living. I didn't need proof from a theologian or a tip from a church practitioner. I needed a piece of a story, something real and full of life and blood and breath and heartache, something way more than an idea, something that someone had lived through, a piece of wisdom earned the hard way. That's why telling our stories is so important.

There are two myths that we tend to believe about our stories: the first is that they're about us, and the second is that because they're about us, they don't matter. But they're not only about us, and they matter more than ever right now. When we, any of us who have been transformed by Christ, tell our own stories, we're telling the story of who God is.

I bet God has done something in your life that would make our hair stand on end if you told us about it. I bet the story God has written in your life and your home gives voice and breath and arms and legs to the gospel every bit as much as a church sermon ever did. Preaching is important, certainly. But it can't be the only way we allow God's story to be told in our midst.

I'm less and less interested in the ruminations of a scholar and more and more compelled by stories with grit and texture and blood and guts and humanity. I'm compelled by stories from everyday people whose stories sound a lot more like mine than the stories of superstars and high achievers. I'm compelled by stories that are ugly at the beginning and then oddly beautiful, stories from around the world, stories that laugh in the faces of gender and racial and socioeconomic boundaries.

I'm not interested in talking heads discussing war and poverty from behind a desk or from behind a pulpit. I want someone to look me in the eye and tell me they're scared, too, sometimes, about the mess we've made around the world and the violence both around us and within us. And then I want that person to invite me down on my knees right next to them, shoulders brushing, listening to one another breathing in and breathing out.

The biggest, most beautiful story in the world deserves better than to be told by the same voices over and over again. I think it's time for each of us to do what we can to speak the extraordinary story of God into life in our own ways, whoever we are—not defined by degree, gender, race, format.

The big story really is actually being told through our little stories, and by sharing our lives, not just our sermons, we're telling God's story in as reverent and divine ways as it has ever been told. God's story was told in Hebrew and Greek, and I believe that it's also being told in whispers and paintings and blogs and around dinner tables all over the world.

When I worked at a church a few years ago, it was my job to help people tell their stories on Sunday mornings at our gatherings. And a funny thing happened. When we were at the coffee shop, when it was just me and them and their story, their story came out in fits and starts, unvarnished and raw. We cried and laughed and every time I was amazed at what God had done in this person's life.

And then almost every time, when they arrived on Sunday, they looked a little less like themselves. They were kind of a distant, polished, fancy version of themselves, and more remarkably, when they walked up on that stage, they sounded a lot less like themselves. They stopped believing that their story was enough, and they started saying all the phrases and quoting all the verses we've all heard a thousand times, turning them from sacred songs into platitudes and clichés. They did it because we as a community have trained them and have been trained ourselves to believe that a story isn't enough.

I could not disagree more. Let's resist the temptation to hide behind theology the way a bad professor hides behind theorems and formulas. We dilute the beauty of the gospel story when we divorce it from our lives, our worlds, the words and images that God is writing right now on our souls.

And let's stop acting as if religious professionals are the only ones who have a right and a responsibility to tell God's story. If you are a person of faith, it is your responsibility to tell God's story, in every way you can, every form, every medium, every moment. Tell the stories of love and redemption and forgiveness every time you experience them. Tell the stories of reconciliation and surprise and new life everywhere you find them.

In one of my favorite Tyler James songs, he says, "My life's not a story about me." My life is not a story about me. And your life's not a story about you. My life is a story about who God is and what he does in a human heart. My story is about the people on my street, the things I read, the way we raise our child, the things I've done, and the things that have been done to me. A story is never about one person. It has a full cast of characters, connected by blood or love or jealousy.

There's nothing small or inconsequential about our stories. There is, in fact, nothing bigger. And when we tell the truth about our lives—the broken parts, the secret parts, the beautiful parts—then the gospel comes to life, an actual story about redemption, instead of abstraction and theory and things you learn in Sunday school.

If I could ask you to do just one thing, it's this: consider that your own silence may be a part of the problem. If you've been sitting quietly, year after year, hoping that someone will finally start speaking a language that makes sense to you, may I suggest that you are that person? If you've been longing to hear a new language for faith, one that rises and falls like a song, may I suggest that you start singing? If you want your community to be marked by radical honesty, by risky, terrifying, ultimately redemptive truth-telling, you must start telling your truth first.

I've spent my life surrounded by deeply gifted pastors, great leaders, and brilliant preachers. I understand the temptation to simply let them continue telling God's story. I settled myself into the back row, certain that a girl like me had nothing to contribute, and that everything in the world that needed to be said was being said by people like them—extremely talented, polished people who never seem scared, who know the systems and the forms and the formulas like the backs of their hands.

But there is one thing that those pastors and preachers and leaders cannot do, one thing they can never do. They cannot tell my story. Only I can tell my story. And only you can tell your story.

This is what I want you to do: tell your story. Don't allow the story of God, the sacred, transforming story of what God does in a human heart to become flat and lifeless. If we choose silence, if we allow the gospel to be told only on Sundays, only in sanctuaries, only by approved and educated professionals, that life-changing story will lose its ability to change lives.

It always goes back to the beginning, no matter how far we've wandered off course. When Christ walked among us, he entrusted the gospel to plain old regular people who were absolutely not religious professionals. If you have been trans-formed by the grace of God, then you have within you all you need to write your manifesto, your poem, your song, your battle cry, your love letter to a beautiful and broken world.

Your story must be told.

epilogue

SPRING

Living through this last season was difficult enough, and then
writing about it felt like living through it again, except that
this time I had to find meaning in it. I knew that meaning was
there, of course, but when I began, searching for it sometimes
felt like trying to find a contact lens in a pool. Possible, but
just barely.

What happened over time, though, what always happens,
is that the process of writing about it healed and instructed
me. Over time I was able to see patterns I couldn't have seen
when I was in it, and I was able to recognize with great clarity
and gratitude God's faithfulness and people's kindness for the
incredible gifts that they were.

I finished most of the manuscript on a Friday afternoon
after two intense weeks of writing nearly around the clock, the
same two weeks that my husband was in Israel and Palestine.
He returned that Friday, and we celebrated our friend Blaine's

thirtieth birthday that night at a fancy party with icy dirty martinis and beef tenderloin.

The next morning we drove to Kalamazoo to visit my grandma. We believed it could be the last time we spent with her, and it was. We visited her on Saturday and again on Sunday, and before we left, we prayed with her, holding her tiny hands. We kissed her and told her how much we loved her.

A few days later, Aaron and I flew to Santa Barbara for a long weekend with our housechurch, one we'd been planning and looking forward to for months. The last time we were all together was at Joe and Emily's wedding, a fantastic celebration of love and lots of dancing. I've never seen a bride and groom look at one another the way Joe and Emily did on that dark winter night.

And over a year later, there we were, of all places, in Summerland, a charming one-exit town just south of Santa Barbara, very near Westmont, where Annette, Andrew, and I went to college.

We arrived late at night, the cool air heavily scented with eucalyptus, and the lights on the hills twinkling like secrets. It was tremendously evocative: every smell and sound and sight reminding me of my time there twelve years ago.

Early on our first morning, I took a pregnancy test. More than one. Positive. Positive. Positive. The happiest possible news. After a miscarriage a year and a half ago and then a long struggle to become pregnant again, it was so utterly perfect to let that wonderful news sink in surrounded by our best friends, looking out on a sparkling ocean.

It felt significant to me that after living through a difficult season, and then in some ways reliving it by writing about it, we were given the incredible gift of new life just as the book process finished. I felt hopeful that as my grandma's life was ending, a new life in our family was just beginning. There was no shortage of connections to me. This felt significant, as news like this always does, rife with implications and blessings.

Just as we arrived back in Chicago, we received news that my grandma had passed away gently in her sleep. Before we left for Kalamazoo for her funeral, I went to the doctor a few times for blood tests, specifically to rule out the particular kind of miscarriage I had last time—that was my fear: another molar pregnancy. The first blood test ruled it out. I felt relieved, beyond grateful.

And then an hour before I spoke on behalf of my family at my grandma's funeral, while they were wheeling in the casket and setting up the flowers at the church, my phone rang. I stepped into a little chapel to take the call. My doctor said, "I'm sorry to call. I know you're at a funeral. But I don't want to sugarcoat this for you. I think you're facing another miscarriage. I'm so sorry."

I cried till my throat was raw, kneeling in the almost-dark on that chapel floor. I told my mom and Aaron before the service but decided not to tell my dad. He was pale and exhausted in his black suit, standing next to his mother's casket, greeting friends and family, and I couldn't bear to ask him to carry any more sadness. When my mom did tell him later that day, he came to find me and told me I should have told him right away, that he never wants me to carry anything this difficult without him. If it's about you, he said, assume that I care, and that I want to know right away, no matter what.

That next week I had ultrasounds every other day, and in

between, interminable hours of waiting for calls, test results, answers. I canceled a trip to Houston to speak, postponed an event where I was supposed to speak to a local group of young moms. Instead I read novels on the couch for hours at a time, pretending I was in Ireland or in the 1920s or Paris, anywhere but here. I didn't answer my phone, but I jumped every time it rang, hoping it was the doctor.

What we learned is that I had been pregnant with twins, and for a small window of time, we knew that one was gone, but there was a tiny chance the second twin was healthy. That was the most excruciating stretch of time, because I couldn't figure out how to hope and mourn at the same time. My mind and my heart couldn't absorb the possibility of both a miscarriage and a healthy pregnancy at the same time, in the same body. I couldn't think or feel anything. And then a few days later, we learned that both twins were gone. When I first found out I was pregnant, the worst phrase I could even imagine was "another miscarriage." Adding the word "twins" to that awful phrase made me physically sick to my stomach.

On the night of that final doctor's appointment, I spoke at the wedding of a friend. I was glad I had canceled everything else, but I wanted, if it was at all possible, to be there for my friend's celebration. I put on a dress and heels, swallowed some painkillers, and Aaron drove me to a lovely old hotel on a river.

Kristin, the bride, was absolutely gorgeous, beaming and dancing before the ceremony even started, wiggling in her chair, excited for it all to begin. I sat with her and with the bridesmaids the hour before the ceremony, all inside jokes and old stories. Kristin was one of my small group girls a million years ago, and now she's twenty-five, marrying Sean, glowing and happy. During the ceremony I read some thoughts I'd written for them on marriage and love and also a blessing, and after a small group picture, I kissed the girls goodbye and sneaked out of the reception, the physical pain increasing as the medication wore off.

As I left, Trinity, one of the bridesmaids and an old friend, caught me and thanked me for coming. I told her I came because of Kristin. She said, you came because it's the kind of person you are. You celebrate the joy in other people's lives even when your heart is breaking.

I'm definitely not always that kind of person. But I felt proud of myself that night, for being able to see outside of my own very real pain for an hour or two to give something important to a dear friend.

When we got home, I climbed back into bed exhausted. In the next days and weeks, I began to find the words to tell friends what had happened, and they cared for us with great attentiveness and generosity. Courtney, Ginger, and Mary came over with pizza and wine. Friends from church and from Grand Rapids and Houston and right in my neighborhood brought flowers, so many that at a certain point, our house looked like a flower shop, reminders of love and hope everywhere I looked. People brought chocolates and soup and bread. They left me alone when I needed to be alone and sat on our couch for hours when the loneliness was too much.

One night I was listening to an Alicia Keys song, a love song. Over and over, she sang, *tonight, I'm going to find a way to make it without you.* And I cried so hard I almost pulled over the car. I know it's a song about a man. But that night all I could think about were those two tiny babies, and how desperately I wanted them, how I didn't think I could make it through the night, how I didn't want to have to live without them. I cried and cried, and when I got home, Aaron and I sat in the dim light of the living room. I told him about the empty, raw feeling in my center. I told him I felt like I'd been gutted.

He asked me what I needed. I rambled and cried and at a certain point, I said I needed the comfort of Christ. We are children of a God who wants to teach us, shape us, and challenge us. But he's also the comforter, the wound-healer, the burden-carrier. And there are moments, like that one, when more than anything else, more than perspective and the promise of maturity and seasoning through pain, what we need is comfort.

Jesus is no stranger to pain or loss or heartache, and there are some times when the only thing that eases the pain is his comfort. I wasn't ready, and still am not, to mine through this experience for opportunities to grow, things to learn, ways to transcend and transform. Maybe I'll be ready over time, and maybe not. But it is an opportunity to be comforted. I'd rather not need the comfort. But I'm thankful that it's there when I need it, because I've needed it desperately this month.

I repeat the phrase *Christ my Comforter, Christ my Comforter*, as a prayer, as a way of asking for help and believing that help does exist. I don't know where the phrase even came from, but to me it's like music, like an incantation, something tattooed on my heart. *Christ my Comforter, Christ my Comforter.*

I wanted, of course, for this bittersweet season to be over. I felt so strongly that when I finished the book, I'd be free to move into another season, one of life and celebration. But this is what I know now: they're the same thing, and that's all there is. The most bittersweet season of my life so far is still life, still beautiful, still sparkling with celebration. There is no one or the other, as desperately as I want that to be true. This season wasn't bittersweet. *Life itself* is bittersweet. There's always life and death, always beauty and blood.

My grandmother is gone. Her funeral was four weeks ago. Those tiny, precious babies are gone, even though I still have dreams about them almost every night. *Christ my Comforter, Christ my Comforter.* I have mourned. I'm still mourning. I don't expect the mourning to be over quickly.

But it is spring, unmistakably. Tender, tentative, just-beginning spring, all mud and young grass and soft afternoon light. It's almost Easter: life after death. The pattern remains, and I'll celebrate the resurrection of Christ with everything in me this year, pleading for a resurrection inside my own battered heart as well.

Spring and resurrection and comfort. A bowl of blackberries, kisses from my son, friends that feel like sisters and brothers: the world is as replete and stuffed with goodness as it ever was. God is present to me, possibly more so than ever because of my desperation, and the world he made nourishes me with its beauty and hope as much as it ever has.

I believe still today what I have always believed: that God is good, that the world he made is extraordinary, and that his comfort is like nothing else on earth.

My prayer for you is not that you live a life that's only sweet and never bitter, but that in even the bitterest of moments, you will find the comfort of Christ, deep and enduring, powerful beyond all imagination.

ACKNOWLEDGMENTS

Several dear friends read drafts and gave me incredibly helpful feedback. The time and energy you put into your reading and comments were extraordinary gifts to me. Many thanks and much love to Emily Gardner, Monica Robertson, Sara Sullivan, Blaine and Margaret Hogan, Casey Sundstedt, Brandy Whitehead, Laura Tremaine, Jorie Johnson, Rachel Connor, Mary Morrison, Courtney McDonough, 'Becca Nimrod, Heather Larson, Lindsay Carlson, Emily Paben, Ruth Olsson, Lori Strehler, Heather Hammond, Annette and Andrew Richards, Joe Hays, Brannon Anderson, Melody Martinez, Amanda Hybels, Josilyn Carlson, Becky Ykema, Laura Ortberg Turner, and Sara Close.

Many friends prayed for me, gave me great advice, and sent fantastic emails and texts that came at crucial moments. Thanks to Kirsten Davidson, Jon and Christina Klinepeter, Abby Manchesky, Julie Lenger, Jessica Yaccino, Kristin Hogan,

Jennifer Schildt, Elsa Ansani, Ginger Roddy, Wendy Lucero, Claire DeLong, Jenny Franzese, Jeff Manion, Brian Johnson, Darren Whitehead, Emily Hays, Angela Burke, and Chris Seay.

Chris Ferebee at Yates & Yates has been an advocate, friend, and encouraging voice. Angela Scheff is a star, and I'm endlessly thankful that she is both my editor and my friend. Many thanks to the team at Zondervan, including Becky Philpott, Don Gates, Robin Barnett, Beth Murphy, and Mike Salisbury.

As always, love, love, love to my family. I'm so grateful to have been born into one loving, quirky, grace-filled family and to have married into another. Living so near to my brother Todd, my parents Bill and Lynne, and my in-laws Dan and Diane is a particular joy in this season. Thanks for letting us stop over and mess up your houses as often as we do.

And to the people who have allowed me to tell their stories, who have laid their lives and hearts wide open because they believe, as I do, that storytelling really does matter, *thank you.*

Cold Tangerines

Celebrating the Extraordinary Nature of Everyday Life

Shauna Niequist

Cold Tangerines is a collection of stories that celebrate the extraordinary moments hidden in your everyday life. It is about God, and about life, and about the thousands of daily ways in which an awareness of God changes and infuses everything. It is about spiritual life and about all the things that are called nonspiritual life that might be spiritual after all. It is the snapshots of a young woman making peace with herself and trying to craft a life that captures the energy and exuberance we all long for in the midst of the fear and regret and envy we all carry with us. It is both a voice of challenge and song of comfort, calling you upward to the best possible life, and giving you room to breathe, to rest, to break down, and break through.

Cold Tangerines offers bright and varied glimpses of hope and redemption, in and among the heartbreak and boredom and broken glass.

Available in stores and online!

ZONDERVAN®
.com

Bread & Wine

A Love Letter to Life Around the Table *with Recipes*

Shauna Niequist, New York Times *bestselling author*

Bread & Wine is a literary feast about the moments and meals that bring us together.

New York Times bestselling author Shauna Niequist offers an enchanting mix of funny and vulnerable storytelling in this collection of recipes and essays about the surprising and sacred things that happen when people gather around the table.

With beautiful and evocative writing, Shauna explores the sweet and savory moments when family and friends sit down together. She invites us to see how God teaches and feeds us, even as we nourish the people around us, and ponders how hunger, loneliness, and restlessness lead us back to the table again.

Part cookbook and part spiritual memoir, *Bread & Wine* illuminates how sharing food together mirrors the way we share our hearts with each other, and with God. And it explores what it means to follow a God who reveals his presence in breaking bread and passing a cup.

For anyone who has found themselves swapping stories over plates of pasta, sharing take-out on the couch, laughing over a burnt recipe, and lingering a little longer for one more bite . . . this book is for you.

Recreate the meals that come to life in each essay with recipes for Goat Cheese Biscuits, Bacon-Wrapped Dates, Mango Chicken Curry, Dark Chocolate Sea Salt Toffee, and many other wonderful dishes. A satisfying read for heart and body, this book is one you'll want to keep close at hand all year round.